Meeting the New

Meeting the New Iraq

A Memoir of Homecoming and Hope

JUMAN KUBBA

Foreword by Mudher Al-Hillawi

McFarland & Company, Inc., Publishers
Jefferson, North Carolina, and London

LIBRARY OF CONGRESS CATALOGUING-IN-PUBLICATION DATA

Kubba, Juman.
    Meeting the new Iraq : a memoir of homecoming and
hope / Juman Kubba ; foreword by Mudher Al-Hillawi.
        p.   cm.
    Includes index.

    ISBN 978-0-7864-7071-6
    softcover : acid free paper ∞

    1. Kubba, Juman.   2. Postwar reconstruction—Iraq.
3. Women—Iraq—Biography.   4. Iraq—Politics and
government—2003–   I. Title.
DS79.769.K84 2013
956.7044'3—dc23   2013027485

BRITISH LIBRARY CATALOGUING DATA ARE AVAILABLE

On the cover: Butterfly flag © 2013 Shutterstock; bombed
building structure (iStockphoto/Thinkstock)

Manufactured in the United States of America

*McFarland & Company, Inc., Publishers
    Box 611, Jefferson, North Carolina 28640
    www.mcfarlandpub.com*

To the generation of my
parents and my grandparents
for their wisdom, hard work and sincerity.
They are the ones who built
what there is in Iraq
today

Contents

Foreword
by Mudher Al-Hillawi

When I read Juman Kubba's previous book, *The First Evidence: A Memoir of Life in Iraq Under Saddam Hussein*, it took me back to a sad time of terror and fear. Those agonizing years, from 1968 onward, touched all Iraqis. Makki Kubba and his wife, Saadya Naiff, were victims of the terrible events in Iraq, and yet they were symbols of courage, sacrifice and resistance, symbols of all Iraqis who witnessed this darkness. I knew them well in June 1986, when Makki Kubba was undergoing treatment in London for physical disability caused by torture practiced against him to suppress his honesty, his love for professionalism and his love for his country. I saw him strong and never failing. He had courage and a determination to confront all sorts of difficulties. Saadya was courageous too, solid and persistent, facing all that they went through with a remarkable smile and apparently boundless optimism. The intelligence unit at the Iraqi embassy in London then continued its masters' "mission" of persecution, and created all sorts of problems for them. Yet Saadya met the challenges again and continued to make life easy and happy for Makki.

Makki Kubba was known for his excellence and professionalism in his specialty, communication engineering. He was awarded many credits from Liverpool University, where he did his studies in the 1940s. He used his intelligence and skill, coupled with a high degree of honesty and dedication, to serve his country. Makki was known for his bravery in raising his voice against the maladministration, abuse and corruption practiced by the authorities.

The consolation for Makki and Saadya lay in their children. Now

1

their daughter Juman has pledged to continue her parents' mission to serve their country and humanity. In her new book, Juman speaks for the goodness of her native country, Iraq.

In reading her draft, I felt the great fruitfulness of Makki and Saadya's upbringing of their faithful daughter, who through her new book has shed light on the grievances of her country during the last 40 years or so. This will help enlighten current readers and generations to come about events which have never been exposed openly in the past, or indeed have been ignored deliberately for political reasons. It is a look at the Iraqi people's struggle through these four decades in the hope of achieving a better life and a happy future. She traces the events from her first visit to her country — her parents' grave, her childhood friends, her relatives whom she had not seen for a long time — to her work in Iraq after 2003.

Juman's writing is completely different from other books on Iraq from 2003 onward. She depicts her experiences with deep human feelings, which one can feel through every word she writes. I expect to hear more from Juman in the future.

Mudher Al-Hillawi is retired from a 45-year career in banking and finance in Baghdad and London; he was also a university lecturer. He is a member of the advisory board to the governor of the Central Bank of Iraq and is chairman of the Iraqi Banks Association. He lives in Baghdad.

Preface: A Word to the Wise

Iraq is headed towards a catastrophe. Not because the American troops have left, and not because of terrorism, or the imported or manufactured post–2003 "sectarian violence." Iraq survived the events of the past ten years, and the horrors of dictatorship and war of the past forty or more years, with pain and agony, giving its sons and daughters along the way, and giving many sacrifices, but nevertheless it is still headed towards a disaster. This course can be changed, however, if wise, sincere and competent people inside and outside Iraq roll up their sleeves and get to work immediately.

Why would I be sounding the alarm and raising a warning flag from the first page of this book? Because the "new Iraq" has virtues indeed, but it also has many vices. The virtues are wonderful, but the vices are wreaking havoc on the present, and unless action is taken right away, they will also mar the future. This book is, first and foremost, a call to the wise to stand up and take action before it is too late. The well-being of Iraq and its people, present and future, are at serious risk of marked deterioration. People's lives are passing them by, and there is much wrong that is frightening to me. It worries me and keeps me awake many nights.

What, exactly, is wrong? Let me tell you.

Every day that comes and goes in Iraq when children experience violence, despair, and lack of a healthy and safe environment is a step towards catastrophe. Every day that people are surrounded by filth and lack of hygiene, have no clean water, or drive on dangerous roads is a big leap toward that bleak future. Days, weeks and months pass by where many children in Iraq sell tobacco and tissues on the highways amidst cars instead of going to school. Pharmacies sell the worst types of medications. Small and medium factories are closing down, and others are technologically outdated or dysfunctional. Agriculture has taken many steps back, to the point where much of Iraq's produce is imported. Young people in Iraq, in their twenties, have diabetes and high blood pressure. Many people in Iraq today still do not know that smoking is not good for them, or they know and they are apathetic. Kids as young as pre-teenagers smoke! There are university graduates who cannot write proper Arabic, their mother tongue. Astounding levels of all kinds of pollution surround people from all directions: for example, noise pollution and air pollution from the electric power generators that are everywhere. The gasoline that is used for cars is the worst type, and the products that are imported from all over the world are not only not of good quality, they are of the worst quality. It's bad enough that we have reached a level at which we import juices and sodas, but what's worse is that the juices and sodas that are sold in Iraq are terrible. All of these are realities in Iraq and they must be dealt with immediately. There are no well-thought-out plans to tackle all these issues essential to sustaining life in modern times. There is only a lot of talk and hype and many pseudo-projects that go nowhere.

Further, today in Iraq, you see truckloads carrying potato chips and delivering thousands of imported packs of chips. And those very potato chips are sold everywhere, but especially around schools. Parents don't seem to know that they are not good for their children. Even worse are TV programs imported from all over the world that have bad language and terrible concepts, all aired with no guidelines whatsoever. I have lived and traveled abroad and have never seen such morally lax and empty-headed TV programs being thrown at people from all directions. All that in the name of democracy and in the name of "the new Iraq"! If we do not begin to remedy these problems, we are nearing the catastrophe with each passing day.

Don't get me wrong: of course I support democracy. I have worked for that cause since I was a teenager. Of course I love democracy, and so do the people of Iraq. They deserve democracy, and they deserve all the best after years of dictatorship and suffering. It is great to finally see that all people in Iraq have a voice, and all of them are counted, and all are considered citizens. It's an important achievement to have elections and freedom of the press. It's good that we have imported goods. We have new magazines and TV channels. People can travel freely. These are wonderful things indeed that Iraqis did not have before and for which we are grateful. I am certain that all Iraqis are grateful and appreciative of their newly found democracy.

Indeed, most people in Iraq speak at length about democracy. From politicians to NGOs to TV program hosts and even little kids, everyone talks about democracy. Everyone in Iraq talks about it, thinking democracy is in itself a *goal*. Of course we all want a democratic government. But why so? Not just for the sake of the name itself, not just so that we can always repeat, "We have elections," and assume that therefore we are okay!

Of course not. We all wanted democracy because of what we hoped it would bring to benefit society. Democracy is a means, not a goal. I am not referring to what democracy means to academics and political scientists, but just to what normal citizens think and expect. To many people, myself included, democracy should bring fairness, equal opportunity, the chance for all citizens to have a decent life, the peace of mind that your children's future is in good hands, the opportunity to say and think what you want. Above all, democracy should bring accountable officials and institutions. Elections and the political process are *means* to achieve these aforementioned things. Just to have elections and have the titles of the democratic process is not good enough. We need to have the substance.

Some might say that I am being harsh with our new "infant" democracy, as is often said in Iraq. They might remind me that there are many wonderful things happening in Iraq and we should be happy and proud of them. To them I repeat: I care deeply about this baby democracy, and I want to be sure that it grows up properly. I want to be sure that this democracy does not let us forget why we wanted it in the first place. And of course I know these ills cannot be fixed in one day and that we cannot do magic. But we must have sound plans to solve these problems, and we must execute the plans correctly, not just spend money and have a lot of media hype.

In the "new Iraq," there are lots of motions but no one knows where to. There are amazing project titles, investments, strategies, elections, political parties, and budgets in the billions of dollars. But these amazing things are not reflected in society's well-being. Astoundingly, amidst all these supposedly wonderful, sophisticated concepts so frequently talked about in Iraq, such as good governance, civil society and e-government, people die from basic things such as faulty electric wiring that is near every house and every building in Iraq. I myself know of one person who died in this manner. He was in his twenties. And I know of a child who was injured in a fire caused by faulty electric wiring. We also hear of hundreds who die or are burned severely while fueling their home power generators with gasoline.

Everyone in Iraq is well versed in foreign concepts and solutions to foreign problems, but either these problems do not exist in Iraq or the solutions are inapplicable. We have, for example, programs that teach people about AIDS, but we do not have programs to teach them about real threats facing them daily, such as cholera, malnutrition, road hazards, sunburn, smoking and others.

The path that this current generation of parents, leaders and government officials pursues today — and I mean everyone, regular people, expatriates like myself and those in the government too — will affect not only this generation but also future ones. Building and rebuilding Iraq is the responsibility of everyone, not just the government. We have no choice but to keep working hard and to try our best to quickly fix things that are wrong.

Yet ignorance, mismanagement, incompetence, corruption, negligence and apathy are prevalent in Iraq and spreading like a disease. Unqualified people are running many important affairs of the country, and that is why we see no results. Of course it's nice to have imported goods. But to have superfluous amounts of all kinds of imported goods of the worst quality is not. And to have these imported items lead to the destruction of Iraq's agriculture and small industries is detrimental to the Iraqi economy and the well-being of the Iraqi people. And of course it is beneficial to have media freedom and to have new TV channels, but why have an onslaught of filthy, brainless programs without the slightest monitoring and government codes or regulations? It is good to use e-learning and e-government, but it's more important to know reading comprehension and writing before moving to electronic anything. And how many homes in Iraq have access to the Internet? And what about electricity? Yes, we use computers today. But how many offices and how many senior staff know about information security? The catastrophe I see looming, having been in Iraq for some two years, is the result of the incompetence, ignorance or corruption of those in many leading positions.

I am stunned by how little people care about doing their work correctly and accurately. And I am further stunned by how they just live for the moment with no vision and no plan for the future. There are no standards for work and no professional ethics. There is disregard for public goods and welfare or protecting public wealth. Even a small family cannot be run in this manner, let alone a country, and a very important one. Interestingly, in the new Iraq, nearly everyone speaks about these issues. Everyone condemns corruption, and everyone asks why the electric power problem has not been solved until now. Everyone complains that although nearly all the sidewalks have been done (paved) three or four times, they are still in a terrible condition, cracking open after a month or two.

But not all is lost yet. There is still room for progress, and there is always hope. I see remaining, yet sometimes fading, elements of reason and fine competence and great sincerity in people who are holding steadfast and doing what is right, whether it is instilling values in their children, doing their job duties correctly, taking care of what is wrong and fixing it, or cleaning up their street. I see those anchors of reason and common good — whether from within society at large, within the government, or amongst the returned expatriates — keep holding on while the rest of the people around them are engrossed in all the wrongs and vices and the cacophony of slogans and mumbo-jumbo.

I very much care about preserving those elements of good and looking after them, making sure they survive in this new disorder that has evolved, accidentally or on purpose, over the past several years. Like a flower in a desert that must be nourished to prevent its withering away, these smart, sincere people must be encouraged. They need to stay in Iraq, find their way to do what they know how to do, and find ways to be supported and heard. This is the only way to get Iraq out of its quandary. Reason must prevail over chaos; sincerity and transparency must win over deceit; knowledge and wisdom must take charge. Arrogant, ignorant people must be uprooted from all sectors and be swept away. Smart and sincere people must stay in Iraq and overpower ignorance and corruption. This is the way for Iraq to recover and progress. This is the way to decades' worth of sacrifices count towards something good.

* * *

But it is not just saving Iraq and assessing its status that I tackle in this book. In addition to Iraq, this book is also about me as I step back into Iraqi life thirty years after leaving it as a child. I convey the mélange of sensations I felt in my body and soul about everything I have seen in Iraq, from the color of the sky at dusk to the way people cook, talk and socialize. And I give my unique Iraqi American perspective on everything I have encountered in Iraq and where Americans and Iraqis are headed. This book links the past with the present and the future. I feel that if I did not say and write these words, Iraq's jump into the future would be like a shot in the dark with no hindsight and no wisdom. There would be a gap in this part of history.

Finally, this book is also a tribute to the generations of my parents and grandparents. They gave today's generations something good. We should all try to do the same for the generations to come.

CHAPTER I

New Year's Eve, 2010, Baghdad

The High Life at Alrasheed Hotel

I found my way to the small, sun-laden cafeteria of the Alrasheed hotel. I sat down in front of the huge window, enjoying my first look at the beautiful morning sun, although it was a cold winter day. As soon as I got the tea that I ordered, it was a reminder that I was indeed in Iraq. The tea was Iraqi style: thick and dark, with lots of cardamom and lots of sugar. Iraqis serve this thick, dark tea in the little *istikan* cups and they load it with so much cardamom and sugar that you can't taste the tea itself. (Iraqis typically use cardamom in everything, including rice and meat dishes.) I had to ask for just hot water and a tea bag in order to have a normal — for me — cup of tea.

That was my first morning in Iraq after many years away. It was around mid–December of 2009 that I came back, this time to stay and help. I had come to Iraq a few times just to visit, and I only stayed a few days then. But this time it was different. I was now back on a mission. A mission of giving what I know, sharing my experience, helping and doing things to heal and help Iraq get back on track. I was glad that I made it at least as far as my safe arrival. I was excited and enthusiastic, but also full of apprehension and anticipation as I began to deal with grounds that were totally new for me, with different sets of rules from what I am used to.

I came to Iraq because I wanted to help and to give my knowledge and experience, to see Iraq progress and flourish and to see good relations between Iraqis and Americans. I am thankful to his Excellency Prime Minister Nouri Al Maliki for the opportunity he gave me to serve Iraq.

I am honored that he assigned me to a high position in his office to participate in Iraq's education reform. I am convinced that Iraq needs expatriate professionals and experts to come to Iraq. These experts are readymade: They do not need training, and they have vision and experience. They just need room to do their work. And then magic would happen. With this in mind, I had extreme levels of enthusiasm and energy. And I, being confident and fervent, thought at first that I could conquer all obstacles of any kind. I was mistaken!

* * *

I got my first taste of malfunctioning things during my first forty-eight hours in Baghdad when the elevator at the hotel broke down. I was in there with three men and the elevator stopped. I and the one foreign man in the elevator looked for some safety button. We did not know what to do. The two Iraqi men were more proactive: They managed to open the door, and we saw that we were halfway between two floors. Some hotel personnel and foreign guards came over to help us. In the end, we all had to jump down to the floor below. I took off my high heels and tossed them out of the elevator, handed my purse to the man who had jumped before me, then sat on the floor of the elevator and jumped the rest of the distance. Knowing that such a breakdown will likely happen again, and that frequent power outages are also likely to strand people in elevators for hours, I now avoid elevators in Iraq. I take the stairs wherever possible.

Among my other first challenges were the times when meals are served in Iraq. Throughout the Middle East, meals are served later than what we are used to in the United States. For example, lunch time is typically between 1:00 and 3:00 P.M. in Iraq. I was usually out of the hotel during that time. I typically do not eat lunch, which means I must have dinner between 4:00 and 5:00. This is what I was used to in the United States. But at Alrasheed, dinner started at 7:00, and I would be starving by then. Some days I went to the cafeteria at 6:30 hoping to find something to eat until dinner was served. There is usually no one there at that time. Most Iraqis eat dinner around 8 P.M. or so. The restaurant did open at seven but not too many people showed up that early. Some days I ordered food in my room, but this service was not always available. Sometimes the hotel staff had to leave early because of some security issue so there would be no one to work in the hotel kitchen. One day they told me that they had no gas canisters with which to power the stove to cook the food.

To solve this food problem in a creative way, I tried to come back to the hotel early enough so that I could catch the last bit of the lunch service. I would arrive around 3:15 just to be able to grab whatever was left before the place closed. Sometimes that worked out. There were no snack bars or other places to eat that were easily accessible to me.

To make matters worse, I did not like the bottled water either. It smelled like Clorox. I suffered so much from the water. Unfortunately, this was the only brand available. Later, some of my relatives brought me boxes of water to the hotel; they brought it from outside where there were other brands available.

From my first few days in Baghdad, I really missed the luxuries of America, where restaurants are open all the time and there is always some restaurant that is open or at least some deli store. Food was indeed a challenge during my first few weeks back in Iraq. Of course, as time went by I discovered many larger challenges.

* * *

The Alrasheed Hotel used to be *the* place to go to in the previous decades. It was where all the posh people would hang out. The people of the previous regime were regulars at the hotel, which was out of reach to ordinary and non-wealthy people. Many people who lived the high life had their weddings and honeymoons there. In fact, several Iraqis I know in the United States told me that they were married at Alrasheed.

But the hotel I saw was the just the skeleton. Its structure was good, for it was rather well built for its time (the 1980s). Actually, it has lavish marbles, exquisite carved wood decorations, and state-of-the-art service systems. But it was barely maintained.

The status of the hotel as I saw it in the last days of 2009 and the early months of 2010 reflected the damage of the wars and the neglect of decades. The hotel was, like the rest of Iraq, neglected and damaged. It was militarized for a few years after 2003. For a while it was off limits except to those associated with a foreign army or embassy. It was still off limits to ordinary people when I arrived. People could come but only if they had access to the International Zone (the IZ), *aka* the Green Zone.

11

But then things eased up a bit and gradually the hotel became more accessible to the general public.

During the time I was there, the first few months of 2010, the hotel was ravished and unkempt. The rooms were filthy. The furniture was old and unappealing. I had to cover everything with rugs that I bought from the hotel store. I cleaned the room and the bathroom before I touched anything. The furniture, although of high quality, was worn out. It had been in use for some thirty years without upgrading. The carpets were stained. It was very unpleasant environment to be in. But this was the only hotel inside the IZ, and actually even other grand hotels of Baghdad were of the same status.

There is a beautiful garden at Alrasheed. It is spacious, sunny and pleasant. It is like an oasis of peace and beauty. People who had seen the garden decades before told me it used to be lovely. The magnificent layout suggests that it was once indeed breathtaking. One can imagine how it looked when the small water pools and fountains were full and functional. There are also a couple of side gardens, smaller and more secluded. One of them is called the "romantic garden." But like the rest of the facilities of the hotel, the gardens were not well kept because of the war events and the militarization of the hotel.

The garden said it all about Baghdad and about Iraq. The structure of things always seemed well built and correctly done. The structure of nearly everything in Baghdad and in Iraq was old but built to the standards and specifications of an earlier era. Most older buildings are well built and sturdy, and they seem to have withstood the hits of time and neglect. But their current status is poor. And people always seemed to remember some good old days decades ago when things were running well. I am referring to things that affect daily livelihood such as buses, trains, and the telephone service. This is also true of ministries, schools, hospitals, roads, factories and other things. Whenever we discuss the status of anything people always say, for example, that such-and-such a hospital used to be good, or such-and-such a factory produced high standard products or made well refined food. Actually, it seems that way to me, too, although I lived only briefly in Iraq. For example, when I was born, my mom went to a good hospital and she was well cared for. I saw pictures of her in the hospital. It seemed nice. The surroundings were pleasant from what one could see in a picture. That was four decades ago, but by standards then, the services were highly praised. Of course I do realize that not all areas of Iraq had those privileges.

These observations and examples highlight the situation of Iraq and nearly sum up its current status. Most of the buildings, roads and rail-roads were built in the 1950s and 1960s, some in the1970s. And then progress halted and destruction began for three decades. The destruction of infrastructure kept on going and was exacerbated by years of war and international economic sanctions during the 1990s. There is marked deterioration of all kinds of services.

But it is not just the buildings and roads that have been affected. The most dramatic impact is seen on society. There is now an erosion of norms and values. There is a "cortex" or an outer layer of behaviors in Iraq that is a consequence of all these decades of destruction. Unfortunately, an environment has been created that does not bring out the best in people. Greed, mere need, carelessness and opportunism have caused some people to become conniving, seeking to reap any benefit from any situation, anywhere. But I never fail to acknowledge that good people are indeed around and they are doing amazing things. It is too bad that wrong and evil are so abundant that we notice them before we even see the good things.

The cortex of behaviors is rather strange: On the one hand, people are outdated in their knowledge and technology, and on the other hand they have become interested in high tech things and they talk about the latest materials that they have acquired. But in addition, people have become manipulative and have developed a victim mentality and because of that they justify many wrong things that they do. Whatever you say to people, they blame the circumstances for it. They never take responsibility for it. Once when I was talking to a lady about her health and diet and the best way to prepare food to protect her and her family's health, she gave me a long lecture about Saddam's regime and what he did to Iraq. She did not want to acknowledge that her lifestyle is harming her health. I talked to other ladies who are my relatives about their health and told them they must take some serious steps to sustain their health. But their attitude was careless; they just wanted to enjoy the moment.

The Iraq that exists today has lost many of the beautiful features it had before. Naturally so: The Iraq of today has been injured, marred, desecrated by the events of the last thirty-five years and further hurt over the past several years in some new ways. I concede that many of the values and traditions have been diluted and have changed as a result of more than three decades of violence, persecution and wars. I think it is only normal that behaviors adapt to the pressing circumstances surrounding people. Just as an example, in some areas in the United States, in response to the recent economic crisis, people's spending behaviors have changed, and levels of crime and marital problems have risen in response to the economic crisis just in a one-year period. Many studies have been undertaken to investigate the effects of the economic crisis on families and individuals in the United States. It is normal. Iraq is no different. Indeed people have changed over the past three decades, but still, most adults who are alive today in Iraq or abroad do identify with what I described. But I know and care about these values and I intend to bring them back to Iraq and make sure that they grow and flourish. I think it is normal that behaviors change and adapt. One hopes that core values are preserved. I am not sure about that. Sometimes I meet amazing people and I feel that good is still alive and well and core values are still intact. Other times I was shocked at some things that I saw in Iraq and it led me to think that not everything is all right. All in all, I think enough of the core values are still intact, but they must be preserved and protected. And this can only happen if corrective steps are taken now.

* * *

I walked in that beautiful garden at the hotel almost daily. It was pretty much the only place one could relax in the ailing Alrasheed. It was nice to get some sun and fresh air. And during those walks I made new friends whom I met along the walkways. And while walking in the garden, I let my thoughts and memories take me wherever they took me. The garden gave me serenity and peace, notwithstanding the poor shape it is in. I found solace and a treasure of sensations in the beautiful garden of the hotel.

There were many kinds of flowers with stunning colors and textures. I enjoyed the roses that were blossoming in the garden. I enjoyed their scent and their colors. The colors of roses aroused my buried memories. Roses in Iraq seem to have unique colors. Roses are gorgeous everywhere, but I enjoyed these roses because the colors reminded me of the garden at our house. The shades of light and intense yellow and light orange and fiery orange are very unique and I have not seen them elsewhere. There were a few other kinds of flowers too in addition to roses. Their texture and colors were so gorgeous. They aroused my memories of childhood and stirred my sensations into a blend of excitement and sorrow. I took photos of the flowers as I did my walks sometimes in the morning or mid-afternoon when the sun was still out. I even loved the color of the soil in the garden — dusty, light dull brown — and the rough-to-touch, crisp grass.

Late February and early March of 2010 in Baghdad marked the end of a sort of mild winter that year which had a few cold days and one or two rainy days. Then it rained during spring, not only in April but also in May. And the spring was in full course in April and May; the days started getting a bit longer, and my power walks turned from pleasure and delight in the semi-cold weather into long magical walks at dusk in a semi-warm weather that gradually became hot. Many Iraqis and perhaps many people reading these words would belittle these feelings and find them trivial. Perhaps they would ask me what I mean when I say that walking in Baghdad in the warm weather is magic. Let me describe this magic.

Baghdad has the most beautiful, captivating dusk hour. There is a magical blend of colors in the clear skies, still burnt gold and sometimes orange-red by the day's sun, with a hint of haze in the air. The stunning gold and blue and sometimes orange colors of the sky mix with the sound of the call to prayer (*athan*) in the early evening coming from faraway mosques and echoing back and forth across the city. It is captivating and stirring to the soul. This beautiful, lengthy dusk transforms slowly and gently into a deep blue sky, daring night. It is sensational.

I was glad that there was a gardener whom I saw often. He did his early evening "Iraqi ritual" of sprinkling or rinsing all the trees and bushes with water. All Iraqis who have gardens at home do that. My dad used to sprinkle the trees, and sometimes we kids did that too. It must be relaxing and soothing — although when I did that as a kid it was just fun to play with water. But Dad sprinkled the trees properly, and that created a cool breeze with a special scent of the dampened trees. The beautiful crisp scent of the water on the trees in the hotel garden was amazingly the same as I remember it. That along with the stunning dusk colors of the sky and the echoes of the prayer call immersed me in a mélange of sensations that were almost hypnotizing. They took me into a magical world of memories and thoughts and infused me with serenity and calm in a dangerous zone amidst harsh realities. During my first few months in Iraq, those evening walks soothed my soul and aroused and shook my memories. It is magic that cannot be described with words.

Amidst all this calm, captivating magic of my serene, delightful walks, I was repeatedly stunned by frogs that popped at me from everywhere and hopped all around me. I ran away from them and screamed at times. The frogs were probably scared of me too.

* * *

Many Iraqis reading my words throughout this book might say that I am painting a beautified image of Iraq when I talk about things I love and I ache to see. I would like to say that not only I am being honest — these things truly were sensational to me and I found true pleasure in them — but also it is my nature to appreciate everything and to find beauty in everything and every condition. It gave me pleasure and delight to see that the color of the sky in Baghdad is pretty, and to hear that the sound of the prayer call is still going on, and to see that roses are as beautiful as ever and as stunning as I remember them. I am privileged to be able to find pleasure in things. I love telling everyone how happy these things make me. And I might add another reason, perhaps, for finding happiness in those small things. It is my own coping and survival mechanism in the harsh unknown — the territory that I was in. Maybe it is a way for me to anchor myself in this new environment; maybe it is reassuring to me to know that if I was here before, I can survive here again.

These walking joys were some days halted because of sandstorms. Baghdad has strange sandstorms in the late winter, spring, and early summer days. Actually these were new to me and I was amazed by the scary, intense change in the weather. But people in Iraq say they have been having those sandstorms for more than a decade. It is a bit unusual because when I was a kid I had seen such storms maybe just two or three times in all of the years that I lived there. And they were different: They had a red-orange hue and were more intense, but they disappeared after that. Today's sandstorms seem to occur more frequently, but they are milder and are not very red-orange; they just have a normal dusty color.

Actually I would have liked to walk out during the sandstorm. But it was hard to breathe and you had to cover your face.

Why would I want to walk during the sandstorm? Because I love to try everything. I would like to know the sensation of the dust hitting my face and how it felt to hide away from it. I also like to do unusual things, and I like to find something new and good in every situation, even one that everyone hates, such as a sandstorm. And more importantly, I like to challenge myself. When I was in the U.S., I used to walk outside during the rain or even the hot weather. I used to walk in the snow and have snowflakes gently falling on my face. I like to try everything. I like to make myself used to uncomfortable, strenuous conditions. It builds my tolerance and tenacity. And it teaches me about myself. However, during these sandstorms it is indeed hard to breathe, so I did not walk.

The one thing I really hated about Baghdad, always and still, is the lizards. This is especially disturbing in the summer. This has nothing to do with the new Iraq. These little creatures were here before, and they are still here in the new Iraq. Iraqis do not like lizards. In fact I can say that this is something that all Iraqis agree on. I do not know any Iraqi who likes lizards.

* * *

All in all, I felt rather like a newcomer in Baghdad. I do not know many areas of that huge city. I only know where our house and my school were and where some of my relatives lived. I do not know my way around the rest of Baghdad very well. In fact, the part of Baghdad where the Green Zone (the IZ) is located is not familiar to me. Most of it was off limits to people during the previous regime, and, ironically, it is now too. It used to be a secluded area where all the government officials and their families lived. I remember passing by there as we drove elsewhere. I do remember the suspension bridge (called the 14th of July Bridge). That bridge is the border region of the IZ on one side. Only people with access to the IZ can pass through. Also nearby at another end of the IZ, the two red buildings that used to be and still are the Ministry of Planning are still standing and still functioning. They are from the 1950s, designed by world-renowned modernist architect Gio Ponti. When I was a kid and we drove by them, they attracted my attention. It is astounding that these buildings are still there and they are functional. They were ransacked after the looting and chaos of 2003, and the news media showed pictures of them burning. But they were fixed and resumed their functions.

Actually, it is kind of weird being an adult in Baghdad and not knowing where I am. I mean, it's okay when you are a kid not to know where you are. But even today, if you dropped me somewhere in Baghdad, I would not know how to get back where I am supposed to be. This is strange and totally unlike me, considering I am quite brave and I can manage pretty much wherever you put me. I have traveled to many countries and cities alone, and even when I was much younger I managed to get around pretty well by myself. So it is unusual for a brave person like me not to find her way around. Well, I am working on it, to know my whereabouts better.

* * *

The early months that I was in Baghdad, several bombings took place. Some were close to the hotel. In fact, the very day that I arrived in Baghdad there were three significant bombings, and a couple of weeks later more bombings were directed against the government's ministries as well as grand hotels. Alrasheed was shaken as if by a quick earthquake. It was rather scary for me, although I had been through several earthquakes, having lived in California for many years. But no special instructions were posted anywhere in the hotel about what to do in the case of such events. One would expect that there would be some signs with instructions telling people where to go or what to do in case of explosions, since they are so frequent. But there was no such thing. It seems that people have gotten used to these bombings and explosions and they just keep going. Before, when it first happened, it used to be that such events were significant; people recognized them for what they are and what they represent and what damage and destruction they cause. But over months of terrorist attacks, people got desensitized to them. I am sure there is no normalcy whatsoever to people who are harmed during these events and that they do remember them with every detail. But it is sad to see that because of the frequency of such events, especially in the years 2004–2008, they became sort of normal.

All sorts of interesting meetings took place at the Alrasheed Hotel. It was the place where all the high profile people hung out, and I got to see many of them by being in the hotel. Companies, NGOs, political parties, meetings, conferences, symposia and some interesting individuals too. I even met some Iraqi Americans whom I knew from the U.S. Lots of schmoozing took place daily at the hotel, even though it was in such bad shape. In some parts of the hotel, where all of these social gatherings took place, the window glass was broken and taped in a rudimentary manner. Other parts were supported by sticks and boards. The furniture was not appealing, as it was well used from the 1980s and was in terrible condition.

I also met some unique characters, all of whom claimed to have come to Iraq to build things and to do investment projects. Everyone claims to be the savior of Iraq. Everyone describes what he or she is planning to do and how important his or her project is to the survival of country. And they all brag about the fact that they met or even just saw some officials. But all that quickly stopped as the hotel was closed down for renovation. When it opened again in late 2011, it was rather nice, but I did not go there that much. The hotel was reserved for the guests of the summit of the Arab League, which was supposed to take place in March 2011, and then was postponed to September 2011, and then was postponed again until March 2012. The hotel and many other buildings and roads were being renovated throughout the period from 2010 onwards. The Arab League Summit did finally take place in March 2012.

* * *

An amazing scene at the Alrasheed driveway is the arrival of the daily bus that takes people to the nearby U.S. embassy. These would-be immigrants come to the embassy for their interviews, and they come as families. We saw this bus nearly daily on weekdays for two or three months. And indeed, many such immigrants have come to the U.S. over the past few years, and I met some of them in the U.S. Some of them adjusted well and others did not. But that is another story, for another book.

* * *

In the IZ there are not many decent stores or restaurants. There are a few places to eat, but they are the hole-in-the-wall type of restaurants. I had to go these places a couple of times, but I stopped after a serious incident of food poisoning. And you hardly see a woman there; all the people who go there are some sort of military types from some country or other, or the others (Iraqis and non–Iraqis) who work in the IZ. They put their weapons on the table next to their meals. I never saw any families there. Nearly all the people there smoke. So even if you go there just for half an hour, the smoke smell sticks on you, and of course you inhale a lot of secondhand smoke.

But this is the least of the health concerns in the IZ. It is not a health-promoting place. When I tried to do some walking or jogging, I was confronted by stray dogs wandering around and live electric power cables lying around on the streets, not to mention debris and broken glass. There is no cleanliness. Filth and trash lie in many corners. But of course things got pretty cleaned up as we neared the long awaited summit of the Arab League. Because of the summit, we got flowers planted in the IZ and some nice fancy marble walkways, although it actually is quite dangerous to walk on them because the bricks that were used were slippery.

In fact I do not understand the obsession of Iraqis — and Arabs in general — with marble floors and stairs. Obviously they look pretty. The problem is they are slippery, and they are used without any sanding, therefore they are dangerous to walk on especially when wet. However, no one really thinks about safety here. It is not like in the U.S., where all aspects of construction are regulated by city, state and federal codes and inspected by officials. Further, it is not just construction projects. Many products here are unsafe: Toys and furniture have sharp edges, air conditioning units cause fires due to electric failure or sparks, kitchen cabinet doors do not open properly, furniture breaks apart, handles come off doors and cabinets, computers just turn on and off intermittently, and so on.

I think people in Iraq care more about the looks of things than their function or quality. This is true in nearly everything I saw or dealt with in Iraq. And this is true in general in the Middle East and not just in Iraq. Just as a simple example, when you go to a conference or a meeting in the United States, the most important thing is the substance of the conference: the knowledge, the decisions, the conclusions. In Iraq as well as in the region in general, the looks and the decorations of the conference receive more effort and attention from the organizers than the substance of the conference.

Many days there was no hot water at the hotel, but (thank God) there was electric power. As I mentioned before, the hotel was poorly maintained and did not have many essential services. Nevertheless it was really the only place where foreigners could come. But the hotel was problematic even for its own employees. And I saw some aspects of democracy in action. There was a strike of employees in the hotel. Actually it was right around election time of 2010, when the hotel employees went on strike for three days or so. They had demands for better pay and better working conditions. During the strike, the hotel had no services whatsoever. No cafeteria, no food, no room service, no making up the room, no concierge and no one even collected the trash. It was really bad. The hotel management had no plan what to do — no alternate way to do the work of the employees. This lasted maybe three or four days. Actually, that was hard for me because I did not even know where to buy food at that time. I was still new in Iraq then. I did not go outside at all. Some friends brought me biscuits and fruits to get by.

* * *

Lives of Ordinary People

I have learned the painful reality that millions of people endure. I knew about the electric power problem in Iraq. I mean who does not? In fact, I have written the last few pages in the cold; the power has been out for several hours. I am wearing lots of clothes, and there is immense noise from the neighbors' generators.

What I did not know was the details of managing this problem for weeks and months and years. People have electric power generators at home and they must maintain them and fix them. They run by gasoline or kerosene, I am not really sure. And there are many types of generators. Iraqis are well versed in the Ampere usage (i.e., electric current) of all sorts of appliances and electronic items. Even kids know these data. The generators are noisy and heavy, and you must put them somewhere outside the home, like in a garden or on a patio. Sometimes there is no water, so people store water reserves at home.

Iraqis have adapted to the lack of electric power that they have been dealing with for two decades. They can cook with natural gas. The shops sell all sorts of Chinese and Korean battery-operated equipment or equipment that can be charged when the electric power is available and can run for a couple of hours when the power is out. Even I bought such items: I have a tabletop fan that can run when the power goes out because it has a battery that charges when the power is available. There are many such items: lights, fans, little coolers.

I do not claim to now know all about the hardship of the current living conditions in Iraq. I sympathize with the busloads of disappointed people emigrating to the U.S. or other countries. Some truly need to restart their lives elsewhere, but others just want to reap some benefits from emigration. While I sympathize with their suffering, I am very saddened to see citizens leaving their country then and now. The circumstances in Iraq were and are disappointing and hurt many who had to leave (in the seventies like my family did, eighties and nineties like many others did). This hurt is still ongoing. It is not an easy decision to leave your home and establish your life elsewhere. I feel sad when I see people whom I met and befriended in Iraq during the past two years and they tell me that they are waiting for the immigration process to go through. I even told one friend that I wished she would not go. But I hope God makes whatever is good for her happen.

I keep contemplating on why this country compels its people to leave. Other countries attract immigrants, and would-be immigrants even pay money to agencies and lawyers to get their papers through so that they can emigrate. Hundreds of Iraqi families want to leave. Thousands left before by choice or were driven to leave by force.

It is not easy to start a new life elsewhere, but people do it because they have to or sometimes they want to. I do not like to see this happening in Iraq, but it is a fact. I have met many Iraqi immigrants to the U.S. or other western countries. These Iraqis strive hard to make it there. Some of them rely on welfare in those countries. Others take simple jobs that they would have never agreed to take in Iraq. Call it adaptation. Call it being realistic. But they do change and adapt. And it is not that easy. I have seen this before with immigrants who came to the U.S. in the mid–1990s and right after the first Gulf War of 1991. It was hard for these people to adapt initially and many of them had to take odd jobs or even had to start their careers over in something different from what they had done before. When I talk to such people they all refer to their children and say that they must secure their safety and their future. They feel that they cannot do that in Iraq, and some are afraid for their children's lives.

How universal this behavior is. It is rather like what my parents did thirty years ago when they sent me into the unknown world, which I think was very hard then and which still seems hard when I think about it today. I adapted well because I was relatively young. Parents want their children to be safe and to survive and have a chance to live a good life. I must say, however, that there is one big difference between today and three decades ago. This time I am happy to say that although there are people wanting to leave Iraq, there are also many people who came back, and they have rolled up their sleeves and started doing many wonderful things to make life better for everyone who is here in Iraq. I do not blame anyone who wants to leave, but I think that those who stay deserve good. It is their right to live decently in Iraq. Why should they leave?

I have never in my life been in such close proximity to lethal weapons. There are so many weapons and armed individuals and armed vehicles in the IZ. Weapons have become a normal thing to look at. Nearly everyone in the IZ has a weapon. It is not only unpleasant and scary, but dangerous, since it seems that everyone takes his power over others by the superiority of his weapons. These armed people are of different nationalities, including Iraqis and Americans. Some worked for the American army; others were from security firms hired by the Iraqi government, and others foreign diplomats. All these people were armed and were so close to where I was. I always worried: What if one of those weapon-carrying staff members of international security agencies were drunk or unstable? What if he were provoked by something and he started firing at us? What if one of these men erred and started firing by accident? What if I or the person next to me just got shot by accident or through the poor temper of some armed man or some misunderstanding and our lives — we the people nearby — would be no more? Men carrying weapons, some hidden and some displayed, were all around me wherever I went. At first it felt like roaming around in an armed militia camp.

Further, during the short trip just from the hotel to anywhere else in the IZ, one still had to pass through a checkpoint. I had to get off the car and be searched, show my ID, and wait in the cold. Sometimes the female staff member who was supposed to search females passing through the checkpoint was not at her post. So I had to wait for her for a while.

These ladies were Iraqis hired by the foreign security companies. We had to turn off our cell phones and remove the battery; otherwise the phones would be confiscated. It was hard for me to go though these motions every day and every time I crossed these checkpoints, sometimes three or four times each way. But many other people did that, too. That was how it was in the IZ. Checkpoints are the norm in Iraq now. Wherever you go there are checkpoints, inside and outside the International Zone. Sometimes you meet some officer who is in a bad mood and takes it out on you. It is hard not to get irritated and upset.

Cars too are different in the IZ. Both Iraqi and foreign officials travel in long motorcades. The cars are bullet proof and designed to protect those inside. These cars are all over the IZ. And although the IZ is well protected and isolated from the rest of Baghdad and the country, before these convoys move around, the streets must be emptied of any nearby people or cars.

* * *

My first New Year's eve in Baghdad — after thirty years — was December 31, 2009. It was an important beginning of a new decade. I lit candles in my cold hotel room, and I prayed and tried to have a happy moment. The room was not pleasant, but I enjoyed my New Year's moment. And it was even more interesting because it was my first New Year's Eve in Baghdad with my husband — a very memorable moment in my life and one of a kind. It was around Ashura, so it was not possible to be festive at all, even at the posh hotel. Ashura is the mourning season commemorating the death of Imam Hussein, the 3rd Imam, in the seventh century. No celebrations or festivities take place during the season. Because that event is observed according to the lunar calendar, the date changes every year; in 2010 it was right at New Year's. Nevertheless, New Year's Eve was special for me in beginning a new year and a new endeavor in Iraq.

When you read my words you might think that I am exaggerating or over-dramatizing my feelings towards Baghdad. But even I am surprised and delighted by my own feelings. This is hard to explain. What I felt when I saw the roses, or when I smelled the scent of the trees in the evening, or when I heard Iraqi expressions for the first time, and all the other things I described, resembles the feelings you have when you find a treasure that you had misplaced or lost or forgotten about or did

24

not even know you had. It also resembles the sensation you might have when you dust off or scrub something beautiful and, seeing it uncovered and fresh, are awed by its beauty and charm. But Iraqis in general do not appreciate these feelings. I used to share my excitement with them, but I stopped because they did not appreciate these special moments and would say that none of those things are as pretty as I was saying.

* * *

My visit to the Alkadhim shrine was incredible. Visiting the holy shrines is an important part of Shia traditions. Shrines are where the Imams are buried. There are many shrines in Iraq. People go visit and pray there. I visited this particular shrine as a child several times because it is in Baghdad. My older brother took me and my sister there when we were kids and taught us the rituals. I also went with my mom a few times. So I know the place well. When I approached the shrine one night after all those years, it was dreamlike.

The silvery glitter stands out in the darkness of the night as you approach the shrine from afar. It was stunning to see, the light striking at me from far away. This sounds unrealistic given the electric power problems in Iraq. But actually the shrine has its own electric power. I am not sure if it is from a generator or some other source. But the bright light outside and the glitter inside were amazing and exhilarating.

What is truly stunning is that the general atmosphere is exactly the same as it was decades ago. People walking towards the shrine, stopping at the entrance to read the script, touching and kissing the golden plated doors, sitting calmly around the shrine praying and reflecting: These traditions do not die. But when we went there many years ago, it was not that crowded — because during the previous regime it was not that easy to go. In fact, it was almost not allowed; it was taboo to go to the shrines. If you went there, you would get into trouble. The regime restricted many religious traditions.

It was amazing. I walked towards the shrine on the very same steps that I had walked on before, decades ago. I saw the ceramic or marble tableau with the inscription displayed as you enter the shrine so that you can read it. I stood in front of it and read the *ziyara* inscribed on the marble (*ziyara* is a script that you read before you enter the shrine). I remembered some 38 years back, standing at the same spot with my oldest brother, who took me and my sister there and taught us to read the *ziyara* when we were little kids. Now, remembering, I was in tears. The ceiling's glittery crystals filled me with awe. The intense light and brightness was exhilarating, breathtaking. The same place, years later, is standing and is as stunning as ever. This longstanding tradition is strong.

Iraqis After 30 Years

There is much that is beautiful about Iraq, about its people and its melody of traditions that has blended millennia of human experience. When I lived in Iraq more than three decades ago, certain aspects of the Iraqi character were unique and beautiful — and others not quite so. Some of these behaviors are the same as before. Others have changed, and still other behaviors are new and have evolved over the past three decades. Some have just recently evolved after 2003.

It is a credit to Iraqis that in spite of the horrible economic situation of past decades, the poverty, and the prevalent death in society as a result of the previous wars and terrorism — especially the death of so many men who once provided for their families — there is still just about enough of the social fabric left intact and viable that if steps in the right direction could be taken, Iraq would blossom and flourish quickly.

In spite of the catastrophic problems that society went through, in spite of astronomical numbers of widows and orphans, in spite of the fact that there were severe and dangerous levels of poverty and despair during the 1990s, Iraqi society[1] never resorted to beheadings, kidnappings, looting, massive corruption, terrorism, car bombs, Shias killing Sunnis, or Sunnis killing Shias. This is a fact that is easily overlooked by everyone who was stunned by the level of violence in Iraq from 2004 to 2008. The fact is that Iraq had no terrorist incidents inside Iraq, nor were there any Iraqis involved with terrorism outside of Iraq. These car bombs, kidnappings, lootings, and so on came to Iraq unfortunately after the 2003 war and have been associated with the war and the chaos that accompanied it. Sadly, none of these events were properly investigated. For example, the bombing of the UN compound in Iraq in the early months after the war went unspoken of and is just one of many examples. To this day, it is not known who perpetrated this event — i.e., who was behind it, who planned it, who financed it.

The good name of Iraqis has been marred by killings, beheadings, looting, and imported alien terms like "death squads" and "civil war" — neither of which, ironically, has a counterpart in Iraqis' daily language, which suggests that these two phenomena were introduced after 2003. However, the imported terrorism and violence did flourish after 2003, and regrettably Iraqis have become involved directly and have supported such crimes. This problem remains a serious challenge to the security forces.

All Iraqis dislike the chaos that happened right after the fall of the regime in 2003. They do not associate themselves with it. They all still ask why and how it happened. They all formulate their own theories about it. No one is proud or happy that it ever happened. It is really important to know the chaos and savagery that we saw in the months and years following the war do not represent Iraq and that these alien behaviors are most likely premeditated and were probably planned by foreign entities.

But for now, let's look at my observations about Iraq and Iraqis after being away for some thirty years.

* * *

Iraqis are fond of talking, sometimes at the expense of listening. Whatever you tell them, either they tell you that they have encountered something *more* amazing or more important, or they declare that they already know about what you just told them, or that they have already seen the same thing you are talking about. Whether I tell them about; American food, my trip to Greece, my scientific research, a book I have read, Thanksgiving, my impressions about Iraq, how I prepare my food, something that amazed me in Iraq or elsewhere, even my memories from when I was a kid — they always seem to know something better or more amazing, or they have already experienced everything I describe.

Of course I cannot generalize about all Iraqis. But this and all my other comments that follow are strong observations that took my attention and surprised and even bothered me at times.

I listen well, and when I see or hear something incredible, or when I do something interesting, I like to share it with it people. But it is astonishing to me that whenever I tell Iraqis about something I get the same response from different people. Either they have seen it, or they just saw something more interesting, or they know something better or nicer. In fact this happened to me many times with Iraqis.

I must say this is really strange and intriguing for me. I wonder why people are like that. They can't seem to enjoy a new story or new knowledge. And this is true also during professional meetings. This is so different from what I am used to in the United States. Americans are excellent listeners. They appreciate new knowledge and appreciate what one tells them, whether it is a new recipe or a new scientific discovery or tips about going to Iraq. They enjoy a conversation and they empathize with a story that you tell them. They appreciate new information and sometimes they write it down and go look it up further. They remember stories and things you tell them. They really listen attentively.

Iraqis also, in general, are proud people. They boast about their accomplishments and their experiences. When you meet Iraqis for the first time and sit down to talk to them, many will tell you something designed to put themselves in the most positive light. You often hear Iraqis say, "I am the first in the region to do this or that" or "The United Nations chose me to do this or that."

I lived in the United States most of my life. I attended one of the best schools in the world, grew up in Baghdad's most posh district, and worked at a high profile government office. I went to the best secondary school in Baghdad. Yet I can hardly talk about myself when I am with Iraqis. They seem to know better and they *all* seem to be super achievers. I immediately noticed this during my first few weeks in Iraq and throughout the months. Nearly everyone I met bragged about himself as if trying to impress me or others. I do not really understand this behavior.

I met many people who talked at length about how successful they are. One claimed that CNN told him he is "the best" and "so unique." Another told me a list of all the prizes he had won in international yoga competitions. Another person claimed that he had won several international awards in the Quran recitation competition. A woman who runs an NGO to help orphans said that her NGO is the only one that is sincere and not corrupt. A doctor I met bragged about his work and his rank and claimed that he is one of a kind in Iraq. I met several students who think that they know the latest in their fields.

As they brag, Iraqis also tend to belittle others. Americans not only listen and care about what you tell them, and give their opinion without exaggerating their skills and their experience, but also they let others speak. They introduce everyone with respect and kindness. In fact, it is very common for people in the U.S. to say they do not know the answer to something and that they are going to find out. It is common to hear humble expressions like, "Let me add my two cents' worth about that subject"— meaning that the speaker wants to offer something simple and acknowledges that it may reflect nothing more than his opinion. Many times in school, in the U.S., professors encourage students to ask any question they like, saying, "There is no such thing as a stupid question." To ask questions shows humility and the willingness to improve one's level of knowledge. Many Americans admit their lack of knowledge about something and find no shame in that. There is nothing wrong with admitting that you do not know something and being willing to learn about it. But Iraqis seem to have knowledge on all subjects, even when they are talking to an expert. No matter what you say, they seem to be able to out-say it and to know something more important and more interesting.

Especially educated Iraqis or wealthy Iraqis (and yes, even *fake educated* and *newly wealthy* Iraqis — and there are many such people nowadays) belittle normal people who do not brag about themselves. Actually, people who do not brag are hard to find. Some people seem to think that if you boast around and if you are arrogant that somehow this indicates you are powerful and important. In fact, if you do not boast around and if you respect people and if you are humble, they see that as a weakness. This is some unique Iraqi complex, and what's really odd is that people respond positively to arrogance and superiority. I am not sure why that is. Maybe it is a leftover of Saddam's times.

Many Iraqis tend to boast about their lineage or socioeconomic background. For example, people talk about their great-grandparents' wealth and fame. Or they think that wherever they live is the most posh neighborhood in the whole of Iraq. And you often hear people say, "My family owned the whole area surrounding the holy shrines a hundred years ago" or "My siblings and I are all doctors and engineers," and so on. Many Iraqis who are from the middle class think of themselves as royalty. Iraqis seem to have an underground "class war" more than the much talked-about "civil war."

Many Iraqis seem to think that they are the "high life" people and all others are and should be below them. Worse, they think that the poor or those who do not come from these "high life" backgrounds are the source of Iraq's problems. They criticize the poor and the less educated and others about everything — how dirty they are, how they speak, what they do in their mediocre professions, and so on. They even criticize their existence as if it is written somewhere that all people should be rich, good-looking and well educated. Iraqis do not accept people as they are. They make fun of people's looks, the shape of their nose, their hair, their accent (dialect), their clothes, everything. Moreover, Iraqis from Baghdad usually see themselves as superior to those from the provinces (the rest of Iraq).

Ironically I see this even in Iraqis who have immigrated to the U.S. and whom American society has accepted and welcomed. Although Iraqis, especially liberal Iraqis, have used the word democracy casually in recent years, they have not truly understood that democracy includes the rule of the majority. And if the majority in one area happens to be poor and not the "high life" people, then the wishes of the poor will dominate. Iraqis want democracy as a nice fancy "western" thing, but they are not prepared to accept that in democracy the poor, the uneducated, the ordinary and the handicapped have equal rights as citizens, that their votes are all equal, and that in some areas they prevail because they outnumber others and everyone has a vote no matter what they look like. I have had dozens of discussions with Iraqis about this subject. They all say the same thing. They blame the poor and the uneducated for the political and economic problems, even though those citizens do not hold any political offices — they are too busy working day and night to make ends meet. And these masses do participate in the political processes that have surfaced in recent years in many countries. Instead of addressing political corruption, nepotism and cronyism in government, elitists just blame the poor and think if those poor uneducated people were to disappear everything would be fine. And further, I am sorry to see that some Iraqis have brought this attitude with them as they immigrated recently to the United States. I myself have heard new Iraqi immigrants criticizing other new Iraqi immigrants, saying they should not have been brought to the United States. Some seem to think that only *they*, and no others deserve to come and live in the U.S., even though all these newcomers came pretty much under the same circumstances, i.e., as war refugees.

In the United States, it is not a crime for someone to have been poor and uneducated and to have later become wealthy and educated after working hard and striving to achieve his or her goals. There is no shame in that. On the contrary, it shows good things about that person. For example, many U.S. officials, CEOs, actors and others came from average or even poor backgrounds. When such people succeed, they are to be commended and admired. Such success stories are often cited as an inspiration to others. In Iraq, on the other hand, people do not accept this hard work principle. They all want to have been born into fame and wealth. People would say, for example, "Who is so and so? He was nobody before. His dad was such and such." And so on. They would cite a person's poverty or simple background or simple profession as an insult. Iraqis do not accept people as they are. There is a strong "class racism," if you will. People brag about their wealth and their special high class background as if they earned it when in fact they were merely born into it. If there is one thing that Iraqis should and must learn from Americans, it is equality and respect for everyone regardless of socioeconomic level, and the need to give them all a chance.

Further, many "liberated" Iraqis — and Arabs too — in general tend to be harsh with you if you are not "liberated" like them, using their own standards of what being "liberated" means. For example, when they see an Iraqi or Arab in the United States who does not drink — like myself— they tend to judge that person harshly and criticize the choice to follow one's religion or beliefs "even in the West." Throughout my life in the United States, I have been able to be myself the way I am in nearly all that I do, and I am grateful for that.

Iraqis tend to boast about Iraqi food being the best. I shall talk more about food later, but just to mention one example that really annoyed me: Iraqi bread. The bread in Iraq is quite all right, but there is nothing earthshaking about it. It is nice bread. Most Iraqis buy their bread freshly made daily from a nearby baker. Not many varieties are available. It is pretty much one kind of bread. It is nice, nothing wrong with it. But Iraqis exaggerate so much about how good their bread is. Actually the bread is the same kind we had since I was a kid. It has not changed. But there are many other types of nice bread in other countries. I have tasted many breads from many cultures and countries, including Afghanistan, China, Lebanon and of course all the nice breads available in the United States. They are all very good and very tasty. All these other breads are fine. And I do not see the big deal about Iraqi bread. But when you say that to Iraqis, they start telling you why they are right.

Further, some Iraqis have the audacity to lecture me and others who came from the United States about Americans and about life in the U.S. These people either have not been to the U.S. or they might have visited there for a week or two during field trips or training tours. Maybe they met one or two Americans. But in fact, these people hardly know anything about the U.S. They may know something very small or brief, but they talk about it at length to people like me who have lived in the U.S. all their lives!

It is also normal for people to talk at length about trips they have made, especially to the West, even if they made these trips some forty or fifty years ago. They tend to tell you in detail about what they saw and all the beautiful items and goods that they acquired from abroad. Most Iraqis respect and like foreigners, but they especially love Westerners and would love to be seen with them and would be happy to invite them home.

I met several people who claim to have met the American military commander General David Petraeus, and that's fine with me. But they all seem to have told the general their opinion about the military conduct of the United States. A few said that they told him what a terrible job he did and that the Americans should have done something different — that they should have listened to this group or that group, and so on. But my knowledge of Iraqis is that they actually look with great reverence to Americans and Westerners in general. I would have thought that if they actually had seen the general, they would tell him nice things about the military conduct of the U.S. and they would have tried to please him.

Many Iraqis speak loudly and with dramatic tone and expressions. People are generally loud, and as you walk into any office people are loud and you can hear them chatting and laughing as you enter the building. And certainly many Iraqis over-dramatize things. Someone might tell you, in a dramatic tone of voice, that he or she could not come to work because of an urgent matter. Then you find out that person simply needed a day off to do some important errands.

I. New Year's Eve, 2010, Baghdad

* * *

On the other hand, Iraqis are generous people. If I want to choose a few words to describe Iraqis, I would first say that Iraqis are hospitable and generous people. They love to be with others and they take good care of their guests. They would welcome you into their homes, spend the time with you, pay attention to you and offer you meals and refreshments. It is nearly impossible to talk your way out of staying for a meal with the people you are visiting. It is really important for Iraqis to serve you a meal when you visit them.

When you visit an Iraqi home in Iraq, you will usually be served fruits as a pre-meal snack or as dessert and sometimes as snacks in between meals. On a daily basis people eat fruits as a dessert after a meal and after tea and as snacks. Cakes and pies and even the traditional Arabic sweets, the baklava, are not served on a daily basis but are served on special occasions like the Eid holidays. In general, Iraqis are obsessed with serving fruits, usually fruits are presented in an enormous amount on a large tray containing a wide variety. Such beautiful trays of colorful fruit are typically used as a center piece of a dining table. Sometimes to show further hospitality, they will even peel the fruits for you — in front of you while you are talking or chatting — and serve you.

One really bad habit that Iraqis have is that they take too many medications. They try to solve all their health problems via medications and not other means such as changing their diet or their lifestyle. If you tell them they have to switch their diet to something else, they say they do not like that food. And they keep searching for medications. What's worse, people share medications. They chat about each other's medical condition, and they take popular medications from their friends and their families — especially if these people obtained the medications from abroad.

* * *

One really exceptionally beautiful thing that I saw in Iraq is how important family life is and what a high regard it has. This is one thing that I am glad to say has not changed since I lived in Iraq decades ago. This is so beautiful and so worthy. Family life is highly valued in Iraq and is the center of people's lives. Families are involved in each others' matters and they tend to see each other often — daily or even several times a day. Although nuclear families have been common for several decades now, it is possible to still see some members of the extended family showing up and around. Members of extended family normally visit and see each other often. One is never alone in Iraq. One is surrounded by relatives and immediate family members. Of course, this means that one is bombarded by their news, problems, demands, and opinions. It also means that one is cushioned by their support and help when there is a crisis. It is kind of a two-way street. After the UN sanctions hit hard — perhaps the mid–1990s — this strong social fabric deteriorated significantly, but judging from the many Iraqi families I have met in several countries, as well as what I know from friends and relatives, I do not think that it has been destroyed. I think this is a typical Iraqi feature, just like the palm trees: being strong and taking many hits and surviving with grace.

Parents are highly revered and respected. Parents are the most important people in one's life. They are the center of one's life. They are the life and the energy of the home. I think this is so beautiful. In Iraqi culture, one always seeks the approval and blessing of one's parents over anything one is doing, regardless of how old and experienced one may be. This is also true elsewhere in the Arab and Muslim world, and I think it reflects Muslim teachings that give very high regard to parents. Treating one's parents in a first class manner is Islam's strongest command to its followers, second only to worshiping God. It is normal for Iraqis, no matter how grown up, to kiss the hands of their parents as a gesture of love and approval seeking. This is true especially for elderly parents. Typically parents do not live alone in old age; one of their grown-up children stays home with the parents or moves the parents with him or her to a new home. In general, the men do that, but it is possible also for women to take that role if there are no men in the family.

Elders other than parents are also highly respected. We never call anyone significantly older than us by their first names. We must say "uncle" or "aunt" as a title before their name even though they may not be related to us. Also, when serving tea or other drinks in a room full of guests you must first serve older people — for example, those who are the age of your parents — before those closer to your own age. If you are serving dinner you would ask the older people to start first (as with a

Free-spirited Dad (top) with his relative and peer during their tenure at the American University of Beirut. They used to study in this place.

buffet). If the elders cannot get up to get their food you must bring it to them. Similarly, if an older person comes in you must get up to greet them and offer them your place to sit.

It is a miracle that amidst all the misery and damage of the wars, the fundamentals of Iraqi society survived. Although on the outside severe damage had occurred, people still kept the core essential values such as generosity, respecting elders and looking after parents. It is true that many aspects of life deteriorated and there was an increase in burglaries, corruption, higher prices, and even prostitution, but society as a whole kept its essential characteristic norms. Although many of the people I met in Iraq tell me differently — that values have deteriorated — I still believe that *core essential* values are still intact, albeit with lots of erosions and rust on them.

However, there is one important caveat. As much as I admire the Iraqi style of family life, there is indeed a downside to it. If I could have my way, I would certainly make military training or some of form of boot camp mandatory for young men *and* for young women. Young men nowadays have become soft and spoiled, and all they worry about is the model of their mobile phone and the color of their car. Girls are like that too.

But let me explain that this is not an entirely new phenomenon. Some elements of it have always been there. Families have always super-sheltered their sons and daughters. The children are at home until well into their twenties or even their thirties. They depend way too much on their parents financially as well as for their daily needs. Moms cook for them and look after them even when they are adults. Their careers are made for them and handed to them. Often they get employed by the government; that is the case for most Iraqis, because the private sector is neither large nor strong. Once they do get hired by the government, they usually use some family influence or connection to transfer their service to somewhere that is nearby their home or somewhere that is more prestigious. Rarely do you see Iraqi youth take a risk and do something out of the ordinary such as start a business, do humanitarian work for free, or explore any other unusual venture.

But this softness and lack of experience among youth has become more prevalent these days because of many reasons. First, because of the availability of private colleges, wealthy parents pretty much can buy their children's education, and these young people do not necessarily have to compete (whereas in public universities, one must score high marks to enter the school of choice). Further, because of terrorism and the lax security of the past few years, many families do not allow their grown-up children to venture out because they (rightfully) fear for their safety. Moreover, since 2003, military training for young men ceased to exist. It used to be mandatory. And I think it should be. Military training or something similar (such as National Guard) surely builds character. But as a result of all these reasons, Iraqi youth are too sheltered. They are inexperienced in real life matters, and they have become soft and naive.

The youth are not self-starters. They do not strive hard. They wait for employment to come knocking at their door. And if it does not come knocking at their door and is not handed to them, they whine and complain about the world instead of making some serious effort to improve their skills or find a job. Just handing out their CV to someone is like a big effort for them. I met many such young adults. I ask them: "Why don't you take an extra course? Why don't you improve your language skills or other skills?" They answer that they are tired, and that all these things are useless, and that they know of so-and-so who got employed because he knows someone in a high profile position, and so on. One young man I met said he is exhausted from the challenges he has faced. He is only in his mid-twenties. He went to college and graduated. I did not hear about any challenges from him. Education is free in Iraq. He stays at home with his parents. They provide him with all that needs! I am not clear on what are his challenges exactly.

Young Iraqis are too dependent. I do tell them that when I was their age and when I was just starting out in my career, I sent out tens of CVs at a time. I never gave up, and I accepted any offer that I received without complaining. That is how you make your career. And what is astonishing is that even the ones who do have a job complain about it. They complain if their job is a bit far from their home, or if it is in a regular institution and not some high prestige place. I met some younger people when I first arrived in Iraq. Some of them I knew from my work, others are friends and relatives. I was stunned by their attitude. Because they had a contract-based job rather than permanent, life-long government employment, they looked down at it; they belittled it. They did not appreciate it. They complained day and night that their jobs were not permanent or were too far from home. They are not self-driven. Although I am much older than them, I have more energy and usually work every minute of the work day. I don't waste a minute, and I do not complain.

Just to explain further on government employment, Iraq has always had the public sector, i.e., the government, as the largest employer for many decades. Not only is the public sector old, it is huge. Most things in Iraq are run by the government. This system has its advantages and ills. It worked rather well in the 1940s and 1950s, producing many of Iraq's seasoned professionals and rewarding qualified people. So in theory it was good. Since the system looked for educated people and put them in the right position, it became prestigious to have a high ranking government position (since it was a sign that you were highly educated).

But this was during the generation of my parents. I think the system worked very well when Iraq was a smaller country and the number of degree holders was normal and proportional to the size of society. Today things are different. Over recent decades, the system has become politicized. Favoritism got in. Forging of documents became common. These phenomena became even more prevalent after 2003, so actually the system today has many disadvantages and has become dysfunctional in some of its components. It has also grown to an enormous size. Many government offices are over-staffed. Directors cannot choose good employees. Further, people tend to abuse this system anyway. As soon as they get in, they transfer their services to some higher paying agency, or to some sector that has less work and more vacation time, or to a job that gives better perks, and so on.

Nevertheless, the public sector is still there, huge in size. It remains popular and highly attractive to young and old people. I do not know about it from experience because I have not been through it. Basically people who graduate from college or higher education or even from high school are classified for their job category and they get ready employment assignments based on their classification. And it used to be that soon after graduation, a list of names was published showing who got hired and where and telling people that they are supposed to report to their work. This system has been going on for a long time. It works well in that government agencies and ministries and schools plan for the number of staff that they need and they just get them. This employment is permanent for life, and it has many benefits with it, such as retirement pensions. Usually people get free real estate, albeit not right away and not all employees at once. Some time it goes by seniority, and there are some other regulations. Also there is a probationary period for these employees, and then they become permanent.

This system has some advantages, but I do not know about them from direct experience. I base what I am saying on my observations of what is around me and on my conversations with many youth who are trying to get employed through this system, as well as with older folks who have been through this system. Today, everyone — and I mean everyone — wants this type of employment and they complain when they do not have it, even when they have other good employment such as with private companies (and these days there are many private companies in Iraq). Most people who do have a permanent government job at some government agency are not even satisfied with that. Their job must be at a prestigious place and it must be close to their house and it should bring them a lot of perks, so usually they transfer their service to some high-life office or neighborhood, as I mentioned, to get more perks or easier work. No one wants to work in the underserved areas and no one wants to work in just a regular office. For example, everyone wants to be employed at certain ministries such as the Ministry of Oil and its affiliated companies because their salaries are higher than those of others or because they get to travel outside Iraq on business. No one seems to choose a work that they love to do.

I interviewed several doctors who were trying to get some training abroad. When my colleagues and I discussed with them their potential employment location, they all said they wanted to go to some well known hospital in Baghdad. No one wants to go to the underserved areas in some provinces for example. I asked these doctors, "You all want to go work in Baghdad? What about the oath you took to help the sick? There are sick people who need you in small remote towns. Who is going to help them?"

Things have changed a bit, now that there are indeed more private companies and even some international agencies. We do see some youth venturing out a little and working at such organizations. And that is good, to try out different things. But even when I talk to such people, they complain about the hardship of such jobs and how far the jobs are from their home and the fact that maybe they have to work until 4 P.M. or sometimes on the weekend. I told them this is *normal* and this is what people do abroad. And at their youthful age they should be bouncing with energy and enthusiasm. They should bear the hardships. This is what youth are supposed to do. This is what I did. But is hard to convince Iraqis. They immediately tell you that their particular experience is harder than that of any other, and they use the words "suffering" and "hardship" a lot.

Many Iraqis follow in the footsteps of their parents. For example, parents who are doctors tend to encourage or guide their children towards medicine and taking over their practice as they age. Parents who are in private business tend to encourage or guide their children towards taking over their business, and so on. In general, Iraqis prefer technical fields such as medicine, science and engineering over the arts and the humanities. There are many talented artists pursuing many kinds of art. But most of them are freelancers, and there is really no such thing as a formal career in the fine arts or music other than in the schools of arts and music. But this attitude towards the arts has changed over the years.

People in Iraq tend to mix business with personal relations. This was true before and is still true today. From what I see and what I remember, business and personal relations are intermingled. It is rare to see things done purely professionally or in a businesslike manner. Often people do business with their relatives. And most meetings or consultations usually begin with personal subjects and do not get down to business right away — Although I think this may be changing with time.

* * *

Many Iraqi women have been career women for some decades. Women had taken great strides in their careers, in all professional fields, before any of their regional peers. Iraqi women have always been the most advanced in the Arab world and even ahead of their peers in many western countries. Iraqi women have been university educated since the early 20th century. Iraq had the first female minister and the first female judge in the 1930s and 1940s, a time when neighboring countries did not even send girls to have primary education. My mother, my aunts and my teachers all went to university in the 1940s and the 1950s. Women in Iraq today and for the past few decades are not and have not been considered a "minority" in science, engineering and medicine as they are considered in the U.S. In fact one of the things that surprised me over the years of being in the U.S. is that women are considered a minority in these fields — and indeed they are. It took me many years to figure this out. It is not the case in Iraq. If you take a glance at university enrollment in Iraq you will see that women are significantly represented in science, engineering and medicine as well as other fields. And I might add, Iraqi women in general are assertive and strong.

Although Iraqi women had always been strides ahead of others, today Iraqi women are suffering the ill consequences of the setbacks of recent years. They have been hurt by very harsh living conditions. They have been afflicted by three wars that took their husbands and sons. Women have endured very difficult lives. In addition to their grief and the losses to their families from the three major wars in recent decades, they have also had to endure all the social and economic hardships that accompany wars. Many women have been forced to raise their children alone because they have been widowed. The men who did not die became handicapped and thus lost their income and their means of living. Women were forced to make do with whatever income they had through their own employment, or to rely on extended family support and even to rely on some of their older children to work. Many children left school because of the need to support their families. Today in Iraq there is a large number of widows and orphans and a large number of young people who quit school at primary or secondary level because they have to work to support their mothers and siblings or even an ailing or sick father. For the past three decades Iraqi women have been tending to their families unceasingly, without a breather or any luxury for themselves. They have been truly and admirably enduring and resilient. If there is one thing that has kept Iraq standing amidst all the grief and destruction and that has breathed life into people, it is Iraqi women.

And as much as I admire and give credit to Iraqi women for all that they have endured, nevertheless, Iraqi women have not changed in some ways. Jewelry, predominantly gold, is still very important to them. They still love gold. The most adored gift a woman could receive is gold. Women typically wear it in excessive amounts — at least that is how it seems to many Americans, and to me as someone who lived abroad. And not just that, they wear these jewelry items daily and sometimes all day long. They wear them at home, at work and especially during social visits and even if they are just going out for a walk. They wear several pieces at once, and the gold items are usually dramatic and big. Gold is not just for women; little girls wear it too, and even infants are adorned with gold. (Sometimes for the little infants, the gold is attached to their clothes since it cannot be put on their body.) Even families who are poor somehow manage to be wearing gold. Actually this gold obsession is not just in Iraq; it resonates throughout the Arab countries. This special adoration of gold pretty much excludes precious stones. Rarely do people like or buy jewelry with diamonds or sapphire or ruby stones. If they do, it mostly means they have lived abroad or they are trendy, Westernized Iraqis. Further, it is remarkable how dressed-up women are at work. They dress up very dramatically with lots of makeup and gold. Women rarely come to work dressed professionally in a business suit. They wear all sorts of glamorous, dramatic clothes.

Although today many women in Iraq follow the Muslim dress and wear a veil, this is a relatively new phenomenon. This phenomenon began in the mid–1990s after the 1991 Gulf War and more specifically after UN sanctions hurt society in a very harsh way. People turned towards religion; many Iraqis started to pray, and women started to wear the veil. Another factor is that although Saddam's regime and the Ba'athists were always secular and antireligion (throughout the 1960s, 1970s and 1980s and prior to the 1991 war and the UN sanctions) and thus few women put on the veil in the 1970s (for example), the regime used religion to mobilize Arab and Muslim populations and started encouraging and even enforcing religion in the 1990s or at least stopped fighting it overtly. So, today most women wear some form of a veil. An equally new phenomenon is that of women wearing excessive levels of the veil such as covering their palms and their face. This too became apparent during the late 1990s, and more so after the 2003 war with influence from outsiders. Neither of these phenomena were present in Iraq during the 1970s when I lived there or during the 1980s from what I see in photos and what I hear from people who were in Iraq then. However, older women in Iraq have always worn the loose, black, drape-like cover, the *abaya*, but this is a very old tradition and the *abaya* is used mostly by older women. But that too has become more common. During the 1970s when I was growing up in Iraq, in a typical month in Baghdad one would see only two or three women wearing the veil and it would have been surprising.

Interestingly, female beauty is defined in strict terms in by most Iraqi men. Here I must say Iraqis are not pluralistic when it comes to female beauty and attractiveness. In Iraq the term "beautiful" is used for women who have certain features — for example, a fair complexion and light-colored eyes are rated very high as beauty standards. Many men are obsessed with light-colored eyes for women — which are somewhat uncommon in Iraq and perhaps that's the reason they are appreciated. Actually I think this goes beyond Iraq and is true for all Arabs in general. Many Iraqi women bleach their hair and make it blond because that too is considered beautiful.

This is very much in contrast with Americans who see beauty in everyone: dark or fair, tall or petite, and big or small. And Americans tend to accept their looks a lot more than Iraqis do. Americans too are obsessed with their looks, but they define beauty in a much broader way that includes many colors and shapes, and they work with their body to accentuate its beauty. Men in Iraq are not free from scrutiny either; Iraqi girls take the looks of a potential husband very seriously. When one proposes to marry a girl, usually the girl is going to complain about his height, his nose, and so on.

* * *

Most Iraqis speak English — maybe not with fluency, but they can get by. Some also speak other languages such as French and Kurdish. Kurdish is also the first language in the Kurdistan region. Other languages are also spoken in Iraq, such as Assyrian and Turkish. Iraqis in general know a little bit about many countries and cultures (of course they do — they know it all!). But they certainly know more about American culture and literature than Americans know about Iraq, even now with the recent war. Iraqis know about American actors, singers, movies, books and cars. Of course they also hold certain stereotypes regarding norms and traditions in the U.S. One could certainly say that the past 15–20 years witnessed a significant decline in awareness of American culture among Iraqis. Again because of the policies of the former regime of limiting exposure to the outside world (censorship, controlled media, and so on) as well as the UN sanctions of the 1990s, Iraq's educational levels and cultural awareness plummeted to their lowest. Some people quit school so they could work any job to make ends meet. And even the credentials of teachers and educators declined.

In this era of modernity and globalism, I did see a couple of young ladies, maybe in their early twenties, walking inside a small shopping center with their puppy. Yes, with their puppy! That was rather an odd scene. (And this was not even in Baghdad.) First, it is unusual to own pets in Iraq. Pet ownership is there, but not very common. I know "high life" Iraqis will jump at me and say, "Of course we have pets." Then they would list the people they know who have pets. I know, and I acknowledge it, but it is not that common. Most Iraqis do not have pets — but the ones who do absolutely do not let animals inside their homes. Some may keep animals outside the house in their gardens as most homes in Iraq do have a garden. It is not considered hygienic to keep animals inside the house. Maybe some people would keep a bird in a cage inside the house. But normally there would be no animals running around inside a house. The scene of those two girls was a bit odd: The two were dressed up rather conservatively (wearing the *abaya*). And, further, they carried their puppy to the car. Now this is very unusual indeed. Iraqis, even those modern ones who own pets, usually do not let animals touch their clothes, furniture or the interior of their cars.

* * *

Iraqi homes are usually big and adorned. Most Iraqis like fancy homes and they fill them with big fancy furniture and ornaments and decorative items. Many people have custom-made huge furniture or furniture imported from Italy. Although there is huge furniture in the United States too, American homes are more compact and the concept of a studio apartment would be very unusual to most Iraqis. No one knows what a studio apartment is. Most likely they would refer to it as a room with its own bath and kitchen. Some wealthy Iraqis have such a room for their servant. Even the average couple who just got married can manage to get a small two or three bedroom house to rent or build — yes, build. Most Iraqi homes are custom built. There is no such thing as hundreds of pre-built homes of the same design as there are in the United States and other western countries. In some less affluent neighborhoods there might be rows of apartments, and nowadays they are becoming popular.

Owning your home is a big deal to Iraqis. Some people have more than one home. People look down at renting very much. They see it as a disability and serious obstacle in their lives. They complain about not owning a home as if it were the end of the world. When I tell them that many people in the United States live in rented homes and apartments and I did too, they do not accept it, and they say, "Oh, but that is different. In Iraq you can't live in a rented home."

But there is a severe housing shortage in Iraq and a new phenomenon has arisen in recent years. Homes that are really large are split into smaller units and are used on a sublet basis. Very often, the gardens are used as lots to build smaller homes — like a duplex — that branch off the main home.

Iraqis were and still are very obsessed with electronics. As soon as a new TV model or cell phone or some piece of electric house equipment has been produced in Korea or Japan, they are the first ones to know about it and they would like to have it. They know the names and codes of the latest models of such electronic items. They usually ask their relatives or friends who live abroad to bring them such items. All that in a country that does not have electric power many hours of the day. Iraqis are also obsessed with cell phone models and they usually have the latest ones. Iraqis also carry two or three mobile phones, and they replace their mobile phones every four or five months or simply whenever a new model becomes available in the stores.

Another thing that has not changed about Iraqis is that they usually don't open gifts in front of visitors. Only those who have lived in the West do so. I open gifts in front of the guests with my western friends or westernized Iraqi and Arab friends, and I wait to open the gifts later — after the guests leave — with my regular Iraqi relatives and friends. I know that in the West, people open the gift in front of the guest to show their appreciation of the gift. The way people show this same appreciation in Iraq is by using the gift — such as wearing it or displaying at home — the next time you see the person who gave it to you. You may also mention that you liked it and that it suited you well. I think both customs are nice.

Gifts in Iraq are usually big in size such as a TV, a dishwasher or something of big value such as gold and jewelry or even a piece of property. Gifts must have a real monetary value, not just a sentimental value. In general people do not appreciate small gifts such as a box of chocolates, although you may take chocolates as an added gift in addition to the big gift. But even the box of chocolates must be big and highly sophisticated. Flowers are appreciated, too, but when you take flowers to someone, they must be dramatic in arrangement and presentation. Iraqis like big or exquisite items as gifts. They do not appreciate small sentimental things.

* * *

Mosques, churches, and all religious shrines are very important to Iraqis. Iraqis are cosmopolitan people. There are hundreds of important religious sites throughout Iraq. These sites are important to many religions whose followers do not reside solely in Iraq. There are many religions in Iraq, although the majority of the population is Muslim. Iraqis respect all religious sites, and they did not desecrate nor destroy any of them. They are all standing and many are still functional today. The average person in Iraq, although he or she may be Muslim, has typically encountered many ceremonies of other religions. Everyone respects the traditions of others. This harmony existed in Iraq for millennia, but it has recently been greatly disrupted by the actions of mafias, terrorists and various foreign powers throughout the years after 2003.

Iraqis are and have always been pluralistic. I am referring to normal ordinary people. Nearly everyone I know concedes that we in Iraq never had this "sectarian" culture that arose after 2003 and has become so defining and even stylish to some. This sectarianism is a new phenomenon and so is the even more talked about "persecution of other religions." I think most Iraqis would agree that we never heard of such concepts before. Such an attitude was not prevalent or open in public discourse as it is now, and it has been utilized to its most potent extent by politicians to reach their end games. In fact, Iraqi culture through modernization passed this stage of social development a long time ago and put it to rest. My experience was the opposite of sectarian. We all have examples and stories of inter-sectarian caring, friendships, intermarriage, the sharing of celebrations, and the commemorating of events. I myself come from such an inter-sectarian and inter-regional family. However, some zealots would argue that we had those exclusionist sectarian sentiments before, that they are our real identity, and that these sentiments were previously hidden because of the regime.

But there are indicators that sectarianism is indeed a new phenomenon. For example, holiday seasons[2] were and still are very beautiful in Iraq. There are many holidays, some religious and others not. Of course the main Muslim holidays are Eid Al Adha, which marks the time of the pilgrimage to Mecca, and Eid Al Fitr, which marks the end of Ramadan. But there are other Muslim holidays too, and many Christian holidays, such as Christmas (celebrated both in December and in January, for Catholic and Orthodox Christians respectively). In addition there are religious occasions for the Sabians, and the main Kurdish holiday, Nauroz, which celebrates the New Year as well as marking the beginning of spring. And of course there are many others, such as the whole month of Ramadan, with its special beautiful traditions and cuisine.

Actually if there is one place in the world where there is pluralism, love and acceptance of others, it is Iraq. A tragic consequence of the 2003 war and the events leading to it — in addition to the tens of thousands of lives lost and others injured or displaced — is the story that has become common about Iraqis, i.e., that we are sectarian people and that religious minorities are somehow abused by the Muslims who are the overwhelming majority. This is a falsehood. Actually, Iraq may be one of few places in the world where minorities feel at home and are intermingled with the majority and are safe. Proof is found in all the multitude of religions which found home in Iraq, some of which exist in Iraq only, and in the many historic churches and current functional churches as well

The generation of my parents taught us pluralism long before 2003. This photograph shows Dad (standing seventh from left) with his friends during a visit to the district of Baashiqa (about 8 miles west of Mosul) in northern Iraq where the Izidi community, a religious minority, resides. It was taken during the late 1930s when Dad was around 19 or 20.

as religious sites that have been around for centuries and which no one had tampered with. Many Iraqi Christians, Jews and Sabians celebrate Ramadan and the Eid holidays with their Muslim neighbors. During the Iran-Iraq war many Christians huddled alongside their Muslim neighbors inside the arena of the holy shrines in Baghdad, knowing that these holy sites would not be targeted by the Iranians.

Not only did various religions live in harmony in Iraq for centuries preceding 2003, but Shia and Sunni Muslims also lived peacefully together as a society. The much talked about Shia-Sunni conflict in Iraq was with Saddam's regime, not among ordinary people. Iraqis were not "killing each other for generations" until somehow the world came to rescue us and bring peace. This is not how we lived in Iraq, and the recent grave events presented a grossly distorted image of Iraq. Even the expression "civil war" with which Iraqis have been labeled for the past several years is alien to Iraqis and when translated to Arabic does not ring any bells.

Yet another example of pluralism long before 2003: Dad (third from left, age 19 or 20) with his friends during a visit sometime in 1937 to the Christian community in the well-known 4th century monastery in northern Iraq (about 22 miles east of Mosul) known by the Iraqi name *dir Matti*.

If civil war among ourselves is something we had been fearing for centuries as claimed by many "experts" and the media, then wouldn't we have heard about it from our grandfathers, grandmothers and elders, and wouldn't the supposed horrors have aroused visceral fear and rage in all of us every time we heard the names Shia and Sunni? But Iraqis do not commonly use the term "civil war." The term was invented by westerners and does not resonate among Iraqis. The only visceral fear Iraqis had in Iraq during the previous era was from the Ba'ath government and what they might do next to the people. Indeed they were sectarian, but not the general public. The horrible violence that developed after 2003 against Shias or Sunnis or Christians occurred amidst suspicious chaos that plagued Iraq and killed members of many religions. The perpetrators of most of these events initially came from abroad.

Today in Iraq most people follow their religious beliefs privately in their daily lives but do not support organized religious activities. It is true that there are many religious figures among the various political groups, but their agendas are generally secular and they do not wish to establish religious supremacy. Even those people who are religious in their daily lives still appreciate personal freedom and do not want their choices dictated by anyone.

Religious practices are still accepted by people and no one interferes with others' religious practices. In fact Muslims and Christians visit each other's shrines and other places of worship. It was and still is common in Iraq to visit a holy shrine and distribute money and food to the poor to fulfill a prior *nither,* which is something like a religious pledge or a vow to do extra prayers or fasting or to give to the needy. Muslims and Christians have always done that and no violence had ever occurred because of religious differences. Moreover, we have a special celebration in Iraqi culture to commemorate the story of Prophet Zakariah when he prayed to God to have a son. He and his wife were elderly and they had their son Yahya (John the Baptist) in their old age. This story is beautifully related in the Holy Quran,[3] and Muslims in Iraq and elsewhere learn from this story and appreciate the patience and the prayers of the prophet.

The celebration is usually held by a family after their prayers have been answered to thank God and to share the blessings and happiness with others. It is common in times such as after recovery from illness or after the birth of a baby to a couple who has struggled to conceive. This is usually a beautiful delightful lunch or dinner party where families gather and lots of nice food is served in a celebratory atmosphere. Iraqis also used to celebrate this occasion further by gathering in festivity at the banks of the rivers all over Iraq, to pray and pay tributes to the Prophet Zakariah. They typically float trays of candles in the rivers at sunset. I haven't seen these events myself, but people still remember these celebrations and they tell me it was beautiful and delightful. These customs seem to have withered away and the commemoration of more sorrowful religious events has taken over (for example, commemoration of the tragic and painful deaths of the Holy Prophet's family while living in Iraq).

* * *

The agony of people under the previous regime as well as memories and experiences of the past three or four decades still haunt Iraqis. And I think the haunting will continue for years to come. People have not gotten over the suffering that they went through during the previous regime. I think everyone needs to tell his or her story and everyone needs be heard. This is the only way to recovery at the societal level.

People talk about their horrible experiences at length. Whenever you meet people, they tell you about their suffering. They remember what happened to their families and their loved ones. They talk about it at length and with lots of passion. And each person seems to think that his or her suffering surpasses that of others — that you have no idea how this person suffered. When I say I know and I care and I understand because I too suffered, albeit in a different way and much earlier than others, they strike back at me: "No, you don't know, you did not see those very same horrible days." I think this is a common response because everyone thinks his own hardship is the hardest of all.

Actually, I do know. Of course I know, and of course I care. I wish there were a forum where these people could document and register their pain — somewhere they could talk about their suffering, describe it in detail, and tell others about what they saw and how much they were afraid and hurting. I know because I was there before. I too was afraid for my life and I too was frightened. And I too witnessed horrors while life was pleasant for many others.

But I also know, not just because I had been there and suffered like them, but also because fear and pain are so human. They are the same for all of us. The reasons to have them and to feel them may vary. But in the end they are raw biological responses that we all have when we are threatened. I know how it feels to fear for one's life because I felt it when "security" forces —*alalmin*— attacked our home in the 1970s when I was just a kid. Of course I know about worry, anguish and panic from the time when my father was detained and we did not know where he was for weeks. Of course I know about injustice from when my father was tortured and harmed and imprisoned.

Iraqis to this day have not resolved how to deal with this dark and terrible part of history. To this day they blame others who did not experience exactly the same pain and fear they had. And evidently each group and each person thinks that their suffering surpasses that of all others. I keep saying to people (not just in Iraq — I have even had these discussions in the U.S. with Iraqi Americans) that everyone's suffering is important for him or her. No suffering is more important than another. Everyone is affected *forever* by these painful events that they witness. And the Iraqi society needs so much healing. I appreciate and care about every story and am saddened by all the suffering that I hear about today. I know how much people were and are hurting. I admire people who cherish these moments and give them their right space and time and also have moved on with their lives albeit with bitterness. Sometimes you don't have a choice but to move on because your have to raise you children or you have to take care of yourself. I encourage people to write their stories or to express them in art and poetry or discussion groups. This is the only way to move on. And it is a wonderful way to document history.

For Iraqis who lived in Iraq during the three wars — the first Gulf war (1980), the second Gulf war (1991) and the third Gulf war (2003) — mention the word "siren" and they can each describe with passion, zeal and great detail the meaning of raw fear and dread. They can tell you about the panic, the sense of doom, the probability of random death and forgetting everything but the people around you in your family and seeking protection for them. They can tell you where they were and what they did to take shelter and how they rushed to find their children or their elderly parents or someone in their family who was disabled or sick. I have talked to many Iraqis (especially women) who have lived through the three major wars, and in spite of all the diverse stories that I listened to — where people were, where they went, and how they managed — many of them said the same thing about sirens. Sirens brought feelings of dread and doom to them. Sirens especially terrified their children. One friend told me something I will never forget: She used to block her daughter's ears because the girl became hysterical whenever a siren went off. Many of the people I spoke to about this who were children at that time said that they rushed to their moms and were glued to them.[4] Sirens and air raids last from several minutes to a few hours, but they were awfully painful and frightening to those who lived through them. This fear of impending doom has marred the innocent childhood moments of many Iraqi children. People who have not lived through such moments cannot even imagine what it was like for those mothers and their families.

51

As I write these words, I am remembering some intense Florida thunderstorms. Magnificent lightning and thunder, along with ferocious rain, went on for a long time, maybe a couple of hours. The thunder was frightening, and in Florida, thunder is like in no other place that I have been to — and I have been to many cities and many countries. Just the mere thunder and rain were frightening and shaking. What is it like when you know the noise is not thunder? And it is not going to rain but bombs and shrapnel are coming your way? What is it like when you smell the burning of flesh and the scent of death surrounds you along with the sounds of screaming and gasping?

Adjust You Must!

How have I adjusted, and how is it that after some thirty years I am able to stay here in Iraq and make it?

Surviving July and August in Baghdad's 120 degree Fahrenheit heat while there is no electricity, and sometimes no water, has taught me a lot about my own tenacity and resilience. I actually made it, to the surprise of many. In fact, I surprised even myself. I did not whine and complain about the lack of electricity and I did not complain about conditions here. I tolerated the situation. It was hard, it was painful, but it passed — thank God! And no, I did not run away from the summer heat. I stayed here in Baghdad.

Adjusting to Iraq after being away for thirty years is by itself a story even in the best of circumstances. Even if Iraq had normal services, and no terrorism threats, and even if I had access to the things that I was used to having in the United States, just coming back after being away for thirty years would have still required a lot of adjustments.

But adjusting to Iraq after thirty years of living in an advanced country like the United States and coming back to an Iraq with such harsh living conditions is a whole other story. The experience gave me the feeling of jumping right into and out of my fears and conquering them immediately. It gave me the conviction that nothing is impossible. Maybe this is how Iraqis survive on a daily basis. I admire that in them — and in myself too, now that I have made it this far.

It sounds horrible, and it is indeed horrible, to have no electric power and no water and to have dust all around you, and to have to wait for a bus or a taxi, and the phone service dies, and roads are blocked, and many other things go wrong. It is indeed horrible to have to go through these situations. It puts you under severe physiological distress to have no water and no electric power in the sizzling heat (and in the cold months too, which was even harder for me as I do not like the cold weather), but I did it. And I am sure it is much harder for people who live here all the time and who live outside of the International Zone. And it is even harder when you are ill or have to take care of some child or elderly person.

Indeed one must have tremendous self-discipline and persistence in order to survive here. One discovers one's limits, one's strengths and one's weaknesses. One learns humility and how to be in control. I consciously control my reactions and try to stay calm and prevent myself from being irritated. Iraqis have suffered a lot from harsh living conditions, in addition to the suffering because of violence and terrorism since 2003 and the horrors of the previous regime. That alone is more than enough. But Iraqis have also endured lack of essentials such as electricity and running water in many areas of Iraq. They also endure bad roads, poor medical services, unemployment and many other problems. It is very hard for people here. But to survive, one also learns to cope, and I did that too.

In addition to endurance and perseverance, one must also have a sense of humor and take life as it comes. One has to adjust and accept things and move on. I do not mean to belittle how hard it is for people here. But sometimes, I laugh at what I am doing. For example, when the water is cut off for various reasons, I use my bottles and small reserves that I have saved. When the water is back on, I rush quickly to fill my bottles. On normal days when water is available, I quickly run to do the dishes because I never know when the water will be out. Sometimes I use paper cups and paper plates to avoid using plates and utensils that must be washed.

Many of my friends and relatives are surprised that I was even in Baghdad in those two brutal months of summer. Many of my Iraqi and American friends and relatives constantly ask me about how exactly I was able to tolerate these harsh conditions. Nearly everyone is very surprised that I made it. Many expected me to give up much quicker, and others are still waiting for me to give up.

Here is how you do it. It is not a secret. I rely on my patience and self-discipline and empathy with other people. I always look at the bright side of things, and I always try to enjoy what everyone just complains about ceaselessly. This works anywhere, not just in Iraq. I can proudly say that I am not a complainer.

I remember when I lived in Los Angeles, everyone complained about traffic and the freeways. Every morning when I saw friends or co-workers, they spelled out their complaints about traffic and how long it took them to reach where they were supposed to be. But I loved freeways and traffic and I still do. And like many Angelinos, I tried to make the best out of my traffic time. While I was in my car, I used to read poetry to myself or practice saying something that I needed to learn, and so on. Here in Iraq, too, I look at the bright side of everything, even the sizzling heat. I tried to find happiness in everything that I encountered. I did so from day one, whether it was the garden at Alrasheed, or the stunning beauty of the sky colors, or the soothing sound of the prayer call, or a warm welcome from a relative and the pleasure of making new friends, or lighting a couple of candles on New Year's Eve. I did my best to enjoy my moment and savor every second and learn from every conversation. I tried to make sweetness and beauty around me. I lit candles. I used incense. I collected or bought flowers and put them where I could see them. All of these things made me happy and relaxed amidst very harsh conditions.

Further, I have come to love the Baghdad sizzling sun. Yes, the very same sun that everyone in Iraq seems to hate. The sizzling heat was very challenging, even to my health, and I am quite healthy. I know it must be really bad for people who are ill or elderly. But I tried to focus on the good of the situation, such as the decontaminating properties of the sun. (Without those properties, we would all be sick from the filth that is uncollected and lies around for days.) I love to have sunlight in my office and my place. I refused to have any curtains or shades installed in the office, and for my place at home, I just had some vertical blinds and some transparent light curtains. The first thing I do when I wake up is to open the blinds and let the sun in. Sunlight makes me happy and relaxed. I love the dry weather and high heat so that I can actually wash my clothes and hang them dry under the sun.

It is not just the sun and sizzling heat that I have come to like and live with. The same goes for the dust. I mentioned sandstorms before.

True, when they happen not only is it hard to breathe and see but also when the storm is over, there is dust everywhere and you have to clean day and night. In fact, in general, even when there are no storms, dust accumulates a lot inside the homes and outside in the patios and walkways. I have come to make myself like sweeping the dust from the patios and walkways, something that Iraqis hate and complain about all the time. Yet I find it to be relaxing and a simple exercise to keep moving. I swept the patio many times and collected the dust in a bag. I tried to cover my face to avoid inhaling the dust. I am sure it is hard if you have to do this all your life, but that's how it is. Just like there is humidity and snow and other weather inconveniences in other countries, there is dust in Iraq. We have to accept it and try to protect our health from it. Perhaps Iraqis will immediately fire back at me and mock these ideas by saying that if I were older or sick I would not be able to tolerate the heat. It is probably true, but thank God I was able to handle these difficulties for a few months.

Further, I also tell people that when I was a child in Iraq before, living in Baghdad's posh Almansour district in the 1970s, we always had the electric power rationed in the summer in Baghdad. We spent the summer months (this happened only in the summer) with on-and-off electric power and during those days no one — and I mean no one — had access to an electric power generator as most homes do today. If anyone had owned such a machine, he or she would probably have been imprisoned or executed. I further tell people that places in the U.S. have the same heat. For instance, summer temperatures reach about 120 degrees Fahrenheit in some areas of the southwest such as Arizona or Nevada, and some homes do not have air-conditioning. In fact I myself lived for a few years in a home that did not have air-conditioning in the United States. Iraqis do not believe me when I say these things.

Clearly I do not delude myself. My enthusiasm and endurance cannot last forever. They carried me in Iraq for about two years before they started to wither away. I always say, and I know for sure, that even very resilient people get tired and even resilience has finite properties. Of course no one can last in harsh circumstances forever.

The other important part of adjustment was getting used to not having my normal American things available in Iraq — things like American coffee or healthy foods like fat free cheese. One temporary solution was to buy what I needed in the U.S. and ship it to Iraq, though it was expensive to ship indeed. Sometimes I paid more for the shipping than the cost of the items. But that solution did not always work. Sometimes the package arrived and other times it got lost, or disappeared and then (maybe) re-appeared. Once, when my package was really late in arriving, I asked a postal clerk about it, and she told me that all the incoming and outgoing mail had been held back at the airport because of non-payment of some fees that the airport charges.

I also brought the stuff I needed back with me when I traveled. My luggage was packed with food items that I like and that I couldn't find in Iraq, such as hot cereal, dried berries, and fruit strips. I even brought my laundry detergent and my healthy cooking oil from the U.S. When I brought these things with me, I had my healthy food for a couple of months. Of course this is not a very efficient way to do things. And I have not really solved this problem all the way. It would be nice to start a shop or a company to import certain things from the U.S. that people need for a healthy diet.

Cooking in Iraq for the first time was memorable for me. First, I would like to say that I had never cooked in Iraq. I was in my early teens when I left Iraq, and although I did do some house chores then, I did not really cook. I was a kid, after all. I learned all my cooking in the United States. I am used to American kitchen products and foodstuffs. In the States, I can easily find fat free foods and whole wheat items and I am used to the food being well packaged and clean. All the recipes I know from my life in the United States need some items that are hard to find in Iraq. Many things we buy in Iraq have to be cleaned thoroughly first. For example, when I buy things like rice or beans, they come impure with things like tiny stones or other pieces of debris. So I have to sift through and clean them before they can be used.

Iraqis seem not to like healthy foods. They criticize my cooking because I do not use salt and rarely use butter or oil. I cut fruits and vegetables; I tell people this is how we serve them in the United States. No one really appreciates that. And people actually are surprised when you serve fruits in that particular way.

One memorable cooking challenge had to do with cooking spinach. I like to prepare spinach dishes. They are healthy, and also they are among my favorite dishes. So I decided to get some spinach. But the spinach I am used to in the United States is the frozen one, or the packaged salad bags. There is no such thing in Iraq. I must admit I had never bought spinach in a raw, fresh, unpackaged form. And the spinach I got at the store was a big bundle with lots of other herbal greens in it. This is how it comes; you can't buy just the spinach part. I later learned from my relatives that is indeed how spinach is sold. You have to buy those other things with it because Iraqis cook spinach only one way and you have to use those herbs too. That was so strange to me. Iraqis are indeed dogmatic and uncreative when it comes to food. They only approve of their way of cooking. Anyway, cleaning and preparing the spinach to make my own dishes proved to be troublesome. You have to thoroughly clean the bundle and remove the dirt and certain parts. It was just a big hassle. So I stopped and gave up the idea.

The biggest cooking related problem I faced is that I love lentils (brown lentils) and I cook them often. But Iraqis do not like them and rarely eat them, so it is not that easy to find them in the stores. And whenever I prepared lentils, people looked at my dish oddly. They did not appreciate my lentil dishes.

It took me a long time to find whole wheat items. Most bakers don't even use the whole wheat flour. My husband and I even asked one bakery shop if they would bring whole wheat and make bread for us. The baker said no one would buy it. We were able to find it in some stores but not all the time. And many times it was old and kind of left over because no one really buys it.

Another food challenge was finding healthy fat free dairy products that are edible. There are some out there in the stores, but many times I bought them and I do not believe that they were fat free. Unfortunately many bad products come to Iraq and find their way to consumers. So I can certainly say being in Iraq was bad for my health.

All these measures I took were the least I could do to take care of our health in this very unpredictable life with no good health care available. My husband and I tried to avoid getting sick by taking all sorts of precautions. Nevertheless, we did get ill a few times. And I think overall our health deteriorated over our two years in Iraq.

* * *

Another challenge was switching between the metric system and the British system that is used in the United States. In Iraq I buy my fruits in kilos, not in pounds, and I follow my weight in kilos, not in pounds, and the temperature is in degrees Celsius, not Fahrenheit. My switching back and forth is still not a hundred percent accurate. When I am on the treadmill — yes, we have a treadmill, and we use it when the electric power is available — I still think it is saying miles per hour and I think I am in shape — when in fact it displays kilometers per hour (less fast). However, I still seem to talk about distance in miles. I have not switched to kilometers yet.

I had a particular problem in figuring out baking temperature in the oven. The oven temperature dial is in degrees Celsius, and I had no idea what temperature to bake at. I looked up the equation to convert the temperature from degrees Fahrenheit to Celsius and did my baking accordingly.

I also sometimes am not consistent in my dates. While I am used to writing dates the American way (month first), in Iraq and many other countries we write the day before the month. So I get confused.

One more challenge: When I sent my clothes to the "dry cleaner" they came back in bad shape and did not look that good. Many of my beautiful suits and dresses were ruined that way. I do not think they dry clean things in Iraq. They toss them in a huge washing machine and then they dry them and iron them, and this is called dry cleaning. After a few times like that and having tried three different shops, I decided not take my clothes there anymore. I know it sounds crazy, but I actually collect them and bring them with me to when I come to the United States and take them to the dry cleaner there.

* * *

My 45th birthday was a lovely day. It was my first birthday in Iraq in *30 years*. It was a rather special birthday because it was my first as an adult in Iraq. I had three amazing cakes that were brought in especially for me from outside the IZ (international zone). There are some amazing pastry shops and bakeries in Baghdad. My staff and colleagues were sweet and kind and surprised me with a small celebration at the office with two wonderful cakes, and then my husband brought me the third cake. I am so grateful for that. It was a lovely day — a very hot August day, but very dear to me. Cakes are fancy in Iraq and they have elaborate designs that I have not seen even in the U.S. Cakes also taste good indeed. I had no problem with desserts and cakes in Iraq.

My first Ramadan in Iraq after thirty years was also very sweet and memorable. Ramadan is the month of fasting for Muslims. My experience of Ramadan was not fancy at all because I was no longer at the hotel and was staying at some place that is called a guest house. It was like a shared home, and I did not have my own place and was not really able to cook what I like. I did not really have a kitchen. (By that time the hotel had closed down for about a year for renovation in preparation for the anticipated summit of the Arab League. But I liked Ramadan anyway. Once again, I tried to enjoy what I had. I enjoyed the peace and serenity of Ramadan. Everything sort of calms down. It was nice that work hours were reduced during Ramadan. This is true in all the countries of the region, not just in Iraq. This is how it has always been. In the sizzling heat I enjoyed my dates and soup and my cold lemonade (from powder mixes I had brought with my American supplies).

Iraqis are obsessed with TV shows during Ramadan. Actually this is not necessarily a very new phenomenon, nor is it unique to Iraq. This is common throughout the Middle East. During Ramadan, popular TV shows include soap operas and some game-type shows (something like the show *Jeopardy* in the U.S.). People tune in and spend their entire post-*iftar* (Ramadan dinner) time on these shows. When I was a child there were some special TV shows during Ramadan, but these days the interest in TV seems excessive and it seems that all people do is watch these soaps and shows. This was strange to me. In all the communities where I lived in the United States, we had nice spiritual programs during Ramadan. We did special prayers and Quran readings, and we spent many nights praying and having the night meal (optional pre-dawn Ramadan meal, some people take it, others skip it) together as a community when time allowed, such as on weekends when we did not have early commitments the next day. What I mean is that it seems we did more spiritual things in Ramadan in the U.S. than I see people do in Iraq.

Further, in the U.S.—and this is a very American thing—Muslim Americans actually do amazing community service during Ramadan, such as cooking for the homeless and doing all sorts of volunteerism, because it is the spirit of Ramadan to help others. I did not see similar things in Iraq. I am aware that there are people in Iraq who do incredible charity work and collect money for the poor, but it is not the common scene. The common scene is that of people who are enjoying their TV shows.

Surviving at the place where we stayed, supposedly a guest house, was quite an ordeal. It was called a guest house but it was nothing like that. Actually I called it "the dungeon" because that was a more appropriate name. One of our friends who also lived there called it "Gitmo," referring to the American naval base in Guantánamo Bay, Cuba, where terrorism suspects have been imprisoned.

It is a big and rather beautifully built house but very unkempt and untidy. It had supposedly just been renovated a few years before, but it was in bad shape. The carpets were stained and the big, expensive furniture was untidy and so unappealing that I covered it with a rug before I used it. I tried to tidy the house up a bit and make it habitable. I cleaned up the common kitchen and brought dinner napkins and new kitchenware. But these cosmetic measures were not enough. Many times this place had no water and no electricity. That was indeed tough. But I survived it, thank God.

But there was a nice garden at the house. As I said before, I always try to find something beautiful in a any situation, and in this case it was the garden. My husband and I used to walk in the summer nights of Ramadan after dinner, when the temperatures dropped slightly. During those enchanting summer evenings, we enjoyed the moonlight and a few stars that could be seen in the dark or deep blue sky. Through all of this magic we were roasting in the dry baking heat. But it was nevertheless relaxing. One has to find beauty and comfort wherever one is, and that is what we did. All these experiences affirmed to me the common sayings that inner calm and happiness are possible in hard circumstances. We also used to walk and jog very early in the morning before anyone woke up. These power jogs refreshed me and gave me energy to deal with all the stress and lack of comfort around me.

That garden, too, had beautiful roses in the spring and early autumn. I enjoyed looking at them and I admired their colors. I collected the flowers from the garden like we used to do when I was a child. We used to give them to our teachers. This time, however, I put them in my room or on my desk and replaced them every few days.

All in all, the story of adjusting to life in Iraq is a long one. I thought

I had prepared well for the adjustment. I have traveled to many countries and have lived in several places. I visited Iraq a couple of times for a few days before this return, but two years down I still find it entirely challenging. All my preparation was not enough. I think I am malleable and I adjusted well to many things. And I think it is brave and admirable that both my husband and I, who had been away from Iraq for three decades or longer, actually adjusted well and did not make a fuss over what people call reverse cultural shock!

My difficulties of adjusting were not so much because of the living conditions. Those were hard but not impossible. The real difficulties began in convincing people to work the right way. I discovered these difficulties progressively as the days went by. And the more I discovered, the more my disappointment began to creep in and it became apparent to me that this "trying to adjust" was no simple task.

Some people in Iraq are resistant to learning new things. They are not open to new, fresh ideas. I met a few such people, and it is hard to deal with them. They told me right in my face, "You don't know anything, you don't about Iraq." Of course I do not know everything about Iraq, but I know many important things. And one of the most important things I know is that I care very much and that's why I came to help.

I also discovered that I speak and write Arabic better than most people I met in Iraq. Indeed, I who lived abroad for thirty years, who did not use Arabic professionally at all in my life before the past few years and who did not learn Arabic beyond secondary school, I write and speak Arabic rather well compared to many people whom I met in Iraq, even those who have university degrees. This was shocking to me. It is the one thing that hurt me most and that summed up for me the devastation of the past thirty years: that many adults, and even those who hold university degrees, do not speak or write correctly in their mother tongue. And this is the one of the main reasons that led me to say that Iraq is headed towards catastrophe.

I love words. I love languages. I love grammar and its complexity, and I love the beauty of words and how sentences fit together. It hurts me very much that Iraqis do not take their language seriously. What's more shocking is that some Iraqis look down at their mother tongue and somehow think that not knowing Arabic means that they are sophisticated and advanced and maybe it can also mean that they know English.

When I told people how important it was to have their reports, their speeches, their CVs accurate and well written, many people were critical of my approach and called me a "perfectionist," although I kept explaining that this standard is not perfection, it is just normal. I explained to many colleagues and friends how important writing and critical reading are in universities in the United States and how students are taught these important subjects over and over in undergraduate and graduate studies so that they can become thinkers and investigators.

Not only were some Iraqis not open to accepting new ideas; they were even more resistant to accepting them from *me*, as opposed to from a Western person. I met many people who were willing to listen to some foreign blond just because she was a foreign blond and not because the ideas were good. We shall discuss this particular subject in more detail in the next chapter.

A Million Palm Trees

Many things surprised me and amazed me during more than two years in Iraq. Many things touched my heart and soul. But perhaps the two most remarkable things I witnessed were, first, the "marathon" or "walkathon" marking the 40th day after Ashura (people walking hundreds — yes, *hundreds*— of miles from various Iraqi cities towards the holy city of Karbala); and, second, the palm trees.

First the Ashura marathon or walkathon: lines and lines of people all walking towards the holy city of Karbala, which is located about 70 miles southwest of Baghdad. These people walk to commemorate this religious occasion. The reason they walk rather than drive is that it symbolizes how much they care for the Imam and his family, that they are willing to walk miles and miles just to reach his shrine.

Custom in Iraq dictates you must stand up when talking to a person older than you or of a higher rank than you. And when you have guests at home you must walk to the front door to welcome them, and when they leave you must walk with them to the farthest point you can, such as their car or the gate of the house. This is beautiful etiquette. Taking it a step further, it is humbling to walk to visit the Imam, rather than go driving; it shows high respect and humility. Further, there is much effort and dedication in this walk. It is a sacrifice to leave your work and daily routine and spend several days walking to another city that is far away. Moreover, it is physically demanding and hard to endure such a walk. And this year in particular, 2012, Ashura occurred during the winter time. So people were walking in the cold and in the rain. I had seen the walkathon on television many times, and of course I knew about it and knew people who participated in it and who have described it to me. But seeing it first hand was very remarkable and amazing.

The devotion and conviction of these people is admirable and hard to believe. The determination to walk a hundred miles, two hundred miles or even more (all from the south of Iraq to Karbala) to go pay their respect and visit the shrine and commemorate this religious anniversary is incredible. Actually it was quite a remarkable thing to see those long lines of moving people. Despite the physical and mental challenge, they were happy and delighted. Just the idea of it is astonishing.

Another admirable thing is their resilience and endurance. These people are no athletes, they do not have fancy walking shoes, but they walk for miles. The closest thing I have seen in the United States is a 10K marathon, but that is not even close. People who walk 10K marathons train for months.. They get support and encouragement from their friends and family. And when they are done they put it on their CV or nowadays on their Facebook page. I admire the determination of these Iraqis — and Americans — who walk for something they believe in. Of course the Iraqi Ashura walk is much harder to do. I admire and salute their endurance and resilience.

Further and also equally admirable is the rest and support "system" offered to the walkers. I put "system" in quote marks because it is the ultimate nongovernmental, civil society-based phenomenon with no interference of political parties. I am referring to the on-the-road support that is offered for those hundreds of thousands of people who are walking by the various neighborhoods that they pass by on their way to Karbala. It is an important tradition in Iraq. Communities along the pathway of the walk (i.e., whose homes are located along the road or nearby the walking path) provide food, drink, lodging and rest cabins, and they take pride in it and do it as families for generations. It is volunteerism at its best. People offer their homes and their food for the walking groups. All along the roads, there are tents, sofas, food stands, families distributing all kinds of comfort items such as water and towels, and so on. This is an important part of their faith, that they are supporting the walking masses. And this is considered a big charity work.

What is really interesting is that whole families, men and women and even youngsters, participate in this marathon or walkathon and also people go with their friends (or sometimes they go solo). There are no government agencies nor companies running these activities. Most are done in an improvised manner. People do their own personal, family and community based micro-planning and macro-cooking and mega-distributing of food and drinks and they provide lodging for free to strangers. It is quite amazing.

* * *

As for the palm trees, I had the opportunity to go to a few cities in southern Iraq by car during my stay in Iraq this time as well as in a previous short visit that I made a few years back. The strip of land along the Euphrates river is a gorgeous piece of earth. As you travel in central and southern Iraq to and from Baghdad — particularly along the Euphrates River, as I did in my trip, but really all over the area between the two rivers — you encounter a special delight, a special scene that no words can describe: palm trees. I saw hundreds of thousands of them. I never imagined that the mere scene of palm trees would be so exciting and memorable and would leave such a pleasant first impression on me. As I remember them now, all I feel is delight and pleasure. Actually, the scene is beautiful even from the plane — as I also saw in one of my trips — and not just as you drive.

As you are driving along you see the luscious deep green color of the palm trees standing with their grace and beauty, thousands, even hundreds of thousands of them as if they were your companions along the road. They were so gorgeous. I loved looking at them and admiring them. I am not exaggerating my feelings at all. There were endless palm tree rows, so intriguing and so graceful. The green of the palm trees was captivating especially as the sunlight of a winter afternoon lay over and shone through the branches bringing soft shade to the ground below. There were palm trees as far as one could see ahead. Something so magnificent cannot be explained in words, but it can be felt and sensed when you are there.

I. New Year's Eve, 2010, Baghdad

The palm trees were alive and standing tall in spite of the death and misery they had witnessed and in spite of the burnt-out vehicles littering the roads around them (I saw that during an earlier trip in 2003; there are not really many nowadays). These enduring palm trees were a symbol of the persistence of Iraq to live, to love and to give. The place just refuses to die. It is pulsating with life.

People who lived there and who know the area well sadly say that Saddam's regime uprooted and burned many of those palm trees and their full forest-like areas[5] for security purposes, to clear the area and keep it from being used as hiding grounds. Still, the remaining thousands of trees are gorgeous beyond what words can describe. And the more I expressed my amazement to our relatives with whom we were riding, the more they repeated that this view was nothing compared to what it was before. They kept saying that Saddam uprooted some thirty million trees. I did see with my own eyes some of those burned-out lands where the palm trees used to be and where only the trunks of the trees are left and stand erect. Saddam did not only eliminate his opponents; he destroyed the vegetation, the environment, archeological sites, religious sites and even rare species of plants and birds.

* * *

With its stunning natural beauty, Iraq could be a paradise indeed. It is beautiful north, center and south. There are amazing areas in Iraq; they just need some organizing and looking after. All of southern Iraq is like a big oasis not only of natural beauty but also of shrines and historical sites. You are surrounded by treasures of archeological sites as well as religious sites. One day when the oil fields of Iraq dry out, Iraq will still be wealthy from its tourism alone. So many people all over the world want to come and visit these places.

I also drove by the desert areas. As for the desert, it strikes you with its stunning colors especially midday when the sun is merciless. The desert gives purity and clarity. I think the desert makes people speak straightforwardly and with clarity. I love the beautiful shades of copper red, rusty brown and orange, and the ease and freedom that comes from looking at the desert, even when you just drive a few miles in.

But Iraqis do not seem to appreciate their desert and its beauty. I tell them the desert is gorgeous and we can learn to love it the way it is.

65

It does not have to be green in order to be liked. I keep saying that we do have such desert cities in the U.S. such as the beautiful Palm Springs, and these small desert cities are gorgeous and lovely. Not everywhere has to be green. For that matter, there is lots of green in Iraq, but that too is not always appreciated.

I also went on a trip to Arbil in northern Iraq. The beauty of northern Iraq — nowadays officially called the Kurdistan region — is stunning. Intense green mountains rise to exhilarating heights. We were on top of mountains and we could see stunning sharp valleys and crystalline water below. The weather is crisp and cold and the air is fresh and hits your face hard. We visited Bikhal falls and Rawandouz resort. The resort is truly a spectacular place. I have never seen such astonishing mountains although I have traveled to many countries. The daring elevation of the mountains reaching high to the sky and the sharp valley below with its sparkling cold water running through were magnificent and breathtaking.

Just stating the names Bikhal and Rawandouz, or *Gali Ali Beg*— the name of a beautiful waterfall — and other names in that area gives me goose bumps and tickles my emotions as I experience intense happy memories. I had one memorable trip to the region as a child. For my own family, it was the only trip that we all went on together. My aunt's family went with us. It was an amazing trip. We had so much fun. My sisters, my cousins and I were young and carefree. Just a short time later, my dad was arrested by the regime, and we were carefree no more.

When I saw the falls of *Gali Ali Beg*, they were as beautiful as ever — strong and intense as I saw them as a kid. The powerful, exciting sight of the falls, with their brilliant whitish color, and their crashing sound moved my soul and shook my stamina. I nearly cried as I remembered my parents and my uncle — all deceased now — and our innocent childhood playfulness there at the very same place. On those very steps my parents, my uncle, my aunts, my brothers and sisters and cousins and I all walked nearly forty years ago.

One can visit these beautiful falls by car; but there is also stunning beauty during the flight from Baghdad to Arbil, when one can see gorgeous shades of green.

* * *

I. New Year's Eve, 2010, Baghdad

As I mentioned earlier, Iraq is a paradise not only because of its beauty, but also because it is laden with treasures. There are hundreds of amazing historical sites and religious shrines that are significant not only to Muslims but to other religions too. I visited the ancient Sumerian city of Ur (about 3000 B.C.E.) and its incredible *ziggurat* (built to honor a moon god of ancient belief), and there is also a site said to have been the residence of the Prophet Ibrahim. Both of these sites are in the province of Thi Qar in southern Iraq. I also visited the tomb and the shrine under restoration of the prophet Ezekiel. This site is important to Muslims and Jews. The site is located in the province of Babylon just south of Baghdad. These significant places are treasures for all humanity and places that I hope many people will visit from all over the world. I also visited the historic city of Kufa, with a history of over 1400 years, and its amazing and significant mosque and shrines. The mosque at Kufa is the first Muslim mosque built in Iraq. It was the intellectual and cultural center of the Muslim state for two centuries.

Many religious sites are currently being renovated and taken care of and supported by services nearby such as hotels and other facilities. It is good that theses sites are cared for, but there is still a long way to go in order to make them accessible and comfortable for visitors. As for archeological sites, they are not up and running yet for tourists. They are mostly deserted. Even when I was a kid these sites were not used for even a part of their potential. People travel thousands of miles from all over the world to take a glimpse at historical sites and at important sites. I am one of those people. The first thing that attracts me in any country are the archeological sites. However, it is different in Iraq and throughout the Middle East.

In most Arab countries, including Iraq, these historical sites are not well kept. They do not have any services nearby: no hotels, no airport, not even roads in some cases. This neglect is not a new phenomenon. It is the norm in most countries of the region. Although most countries of the Middle East have amazing, breathtaking archeological sites, most local people are not interested in going to see them, and governments also ignore the potential use of these sites for tourism and even educational purposes. Maybe the only exception to that is Egypt, where millions of people visit the country because of its history. Egypt has been accessible to people from various countries. There are many tourists and there are

The *Gali Ali Beg* falls in northern Iraq in the Kurdistan region, as stunning and intense as I remember them from some forty years ago when I went there with my family on a trip.

adequate services for them. The attitude of neglecting archeology and history has just changed recently, maybe over the past nine or ten years, where in some nearby countries historical, archeological and ecological sites are being taken care of and services and roads have recently been provided.

Iraqis in general and even people in neighboring countries do not appreciate the archeological treasures that they have or even those of other countries. They are more interested in shopping malls and new cars. In fact, on a trip to Syria a few years back, both my husband and I were very eager to visit the ruins of the ancient city of Palmyra. We asked the hotel to arrange such a trip for us. So they arranged for a car and a driver to take us and bring us back on the same day. It was about a three-hour drive from Damascus towards the desert. The driver was very surprised that we spoke Arabic and that we came from Iraq. He said he was expecting foreigners and that in all his experience at the hotel, he never took any Arabs to Palmyra. He said no one cares to go there. And when we went, it was a long drive and the roads were barely paved. As I mentioned, only in recent years have several countries begun to take care of these tourist attractions. On the three-hour drive to Palmyra, there was one small shop and rest area. We stopped there to get water and souvenirs.

Back in Iraq, I was grateful to see the gorgeous and significant historical and archeological sites. And I was thrilled to have gotten the opportunity to see those places once. I kept telling my relatives and friends how amazed I was and that if such things were in the U.S., the citizens and the authorities would have taken great care of them and would have appreciated them.

As we drove to various cities I also saw shocking scenes: older women carrying heavy items walking long distances along the freeway; young kids selling gasoline in buckets on the roadsides; roads in terrible conditions, maybe from overuse and lack of maintenance and also from all the armored traffic. In small run-down cities just south of Baghdad, people looked tired and drained with so many burdens on their shoulders and so much agony in their souls. I saw muddy unpaved roads, run-down buildings, old shops nearly collapsing and cars from the 1970s still running. I saw homes so simple they barely provide a shelter for those who inhabit them. Built of mud and bricks, they were barely standing. Other homes I saw were better built but so old they too were nearly collapsing, and it looked as if they had never been maintained or renovated. It was evident that decades of neglect upon neglect led to these conditions. These things did not just happen after the 2003 war and after the regime collapsed. This had been the case for decades in southern Iraq. It was just another form of hatred or discrimination that Saddam used against the people. It is apparent that humanity has been neglected in Iraq, that people have been suffering and that I was seeing external symptoms of long-standing and serious underlying neglect and abandonment. It turns out the regime had neglected many parts of the Iraq. Later I learned other areas were also neglected.

In addition to not paying attention to archeological sites, it is common throughout the Middle East that capital cities take the lion's share of the countries' developmental and construction resources. This tendency is evident throughout the Middle East where the capital cities have some glamour and developed areas. Perhaps this is one reason for such neglect that I saw in Iraq. But this only accounts for a part of the story. Saddam's regime depleted the resources of the country for the ruler's own pleasure and prosperity. They built gigantic ornamented palaces and homes for themselves and their family members while the rest of the country was suffering. Areas of Iraq other than Baghdad were very underdeveloped compared to the capital city, which is where I had lived when I was young. Baghdad was an amazing city in the 1970s, with many lavish areas.

But neglect is not the whole story. Throughout the mid–1990s and until 2003, severe poverty hit Iraq. This poverty was due to the aftermath of the Gulf War of 1991 and the subsequent economic sanctions imposed by the United Nations. It is important to know about these UN sanctions in order to understand the severe levels of decay that occurred in Iraq. It is no exaggeration to say that in Iraq's recent history (the past 50 years or so) no event has caused more damage that the economic sanctions. The sanctions harmed everyone in Iraq except Saddam and his followers. During that decade of sanctions the middle class was annihilated and it became hard for ordinary working people to survive. Many of them became poor when they had never known poverty before. Many nice places and facilities such as hospitals, libraries, and roads deteriorated during that period due to lack of materials to supply and repair these facilities. These very poor economic conditions caused not only the decay of the existing infrastructure but, even more, the decay of the social fabric. I heard stories about a new phenomenon that arose during the 1990s: Infants were abandoned at the doorsteps of hospitals and mosques in the hope that someone would care for them. This had been previously unheard of in Iraq. People started to sell their luxurious items such as jewelry and cars so that they could have money to survive.[6] The seeds of many of the phenomena I allude to throughout this book, such as corruption and greed, were planted during the time of the UN economic sanctions.

But I end this chapter on a happy note. All along these underdeveloped areas I saw children playing and cheering and having a good time despite the terrible conditions surrounding them. These kids are happy, and I and others shall work hard to ensure that their future is sound.

Like many, I thought the answer lies in a democratic regime. I thought it was a process, a practice and a means to achieve societal aims — not aims of political parties. But in Iraq, even democracy is not what it should be.

Notes

1. The regime of Saddam Hussein terrorized and killed and maimed his opponents using some of these methods, but there were no acts of terrorism or kidnappings by mafias and extremist organizations such as we have seen in recent years.

2. "Holiday season" in the U.S. often refers to religious holidays. In Iraq the equivalent term is *Alayad* which means religious celebrations and also could be used for non-religious celebrations.

3. You may read the text in the Holy Quran in a chapter called *Surat Maryam* (Mary) and *Surat Al Imran* (The House of Imran).

4. As I listened to many of these people — mostly women friends and relatives — they all remembered precisely how they tended to their family members. Indeed that is what women do during panic and crises. They do not run for their lives. They run to shelter those around them: a child, an infant, an elderly parent. It is interesting to me as a scientist that this sheltering and caring behavior, which women typically display during crises, even has scientific significance.

5. The correct Arabic word that is used for these mini-forest-like gardens is *bustan*. *Bustan* is a large garden that may be surrounded by a fence or a high wall. It is used primarily for leisure and as an asset, not as much for commercial production of fruit although it may produce fruit for personal or local consumption. It is not a typical garden; it is larger and denser than a garden would be. It typically

has palms and other fruit bearing trees which are usually planted near the palm trees. They are referred to in the plural form as *basatin alnakhal,* which means the palm gardens.

6. Much literature is available on the effects of the sanctions. One important source is "Health Effects of Sanctions on Iraq," *The Lancet,* vol. 346 (December 2, 1995), p. 1439.

CHAPTER II

What Does "Democracy" Mean?

Hope

The story of Iraq did not begin in 2003 nor in 1991, the two dates pertaining to Iraq that are important for the world community and for the United States because they involved western and international military actions in Iraq. Events preceding these dates by many years are the roots of this story as well as the policies of the world community, including the United States, over four decades. That is where this story begins. We must consider these parts of history in order to understand what is happening today.

The destruction of Iraq did not take place during the war of 2003. The real destruction of Iraq is what happened over the three decades before the war. Some thirty years of repressive totalitarian rule during which the very same world community that is in Iraq today actually helped Saddam's regime.

Decades before the onset of the 2003 war, Saddam's regime had already damaged Iraq and had already inflicted boundless pain and suffering on Iraq as a country, as a people and as a society. Over a period of three decades, Saddam had led his country into a muddle. By the 2003 war, the persecution and severe lack of human rights and the tremendous abuses of the regime had touched nearly everyone in Iraq. Thousands of people perished in the torture dungeons. Others were executed out in the public arenas, their bodies left out in the street. The political struggle against Saddam consumed many brave Iraqis in a savage and cruel onslaught over a period of three decades.

Those who did not die had it even worse. They were severely

restricted in what they could do. They had to obey the regime in every-thing. They had to accept what was given to them without question. And if they dared say something critical of the government, they were severely punished. People were afraid to talk and afraid to criticize the government. Maybe some people were even afraid to think about those things.

These horrors were further compounded by the effects of the first two Gulf wars, the Iran–Iraq war and the 1991 Gulf War. The economic situation had gone so bad that there were people living in severe poverty, having to sell everything they owned from jewelry to cars to furniture to computers, even to their own body organs, to make a living. Actually in our contemporary history few had seen poverty in Iraq until after the 1991 war and the UN sanctions that followed. That war destroyed many important segments of the infrastructure all over Iraq. And since that time many roads, bridges and plants have become dysfunctional. Although some were repaired, the overall infrastructure remains weak. These difficulties have made life so hard for Iraqis.

At some point in the 1990s, especially for those of us who had spent many years of their lives opposing the Iraqi regime, it almost seemed impossible that Saddam's regime would go away one day. Some among us thought that would never happen. So many years of opposition to that regime and so many lives lost in Iraq in the 1970s, 1980s, and 1990s — all to no avail. So many disappointments at the international community and its policies towards Iraq which always brought bad consequences to the people of Iraq. Notwithstanding one's support or opposition to the Iraq war, the removal of Saddam's regime was a good thing. It is only fair to say that nearly all Iraqis were and still are grateful to the United States for the removal of Saddam's regime even though they vehemently oppose what happened afterwards.

Iraqis had hoped that things would change for the better. That hope had nothing to do with the war itself. Iraqis had aspired to regime change for many years; not only that, but they worked hard for it. They struggled for many years, and many people gave their lives for that cause. That hope for a better regime was planted over the years by the thousands of dissidents who struggled and sometimes gave their lives so that others might have a better chance to live and the road could be open for all. And that hope seemed vindicated during the war when the regime of Saddam

II. What Does "Democracy" Mean?

Hussein crumbled so quickly in April 2003. It was a long awaited goal finally reached, albeit via different means. One could finally see the end of this regime and the beginning of a new life in Iraq. One could finally breathe and think freely. One could finally live free.

All Iraqis had their hopes sky-high and thought that things would get better, not just politically, but also in every way. In addition to freedom, everyone thought that there would be qualified staff running services and daily living problems would be solved. After all, it was Saddam's regime that was the obstacle to progress and prosperity.

Many people supported the 2003 war and others opposed it. The sharp dichotomy of opinions for and against the war was prevalent not just in Iraq but also in the United States and other countries that participated in the war. Nevertheless, most if not all Iraqis, both at home and abroad, were happy to see the statue of Saddam come down. Finally a breath of air and a new light had come to Iraq after decades of repression.

The "intelligentsia" abroad, those all too well-known chic expatriate Iraqis who thought of themselves as the future leaders of Iraq, thought that this window of opportunity would let them have a go and bring in qualified good people to run the country. These guys were ready to jump in and fill the scene in Iraq. Most of them hoped for high government posts for themselves.

For a few weeks and months things appeared on the outside to be going all right. Many expatriate Iraqis went back to Iraq for the first time in decades and visited their relatives whom they had not seen in years. That was a truly important milestone for them and their families. There were many joyous moments of family reunion. Many books could be written about these experiences. Some people had left Iraq in the seventies, the eighties and the nineties. Some of them had not seen their families for over two or three decades. For some, ailing parents had passed away and a new generation of relatives had been born and raised. No one could travel normally during Saddam's time. Going out of Iraq was nearly impossible. Going into Iraq during Saddam's time — for those of us who were abroad — was frightening and dangerous if not impossible. These were cruel and harsh years for many Iraqis.

After the collapse of the regime, people talked freely among themselves for the first time in decades. And later when the phones were running, people spoke freely on the phone. During Saddam's era, the phones were tapped and people had to speak very cautiously using coded messages. Even then they were punished or arrested as a result.

Also for the first time in decades, various goods became available in the shops, although they were still expensive and unaffordable for most people. All of a sudden many Iraqi TV channels (via satellite) were running and offering all kinds of shows. Magazines and books were available in the bookshops. Dozens of TV channels, magazines, and newspapers sprang out quickly and today there are huge numbers of them. Some of them are good and others terrible. Some of them exclusively represent certain political parties and they just propagate those agendas. They are loaded with ideas, expressions and slogans it's as though everyone wanted to say something and be heard, and now there seems to be a media outlet for everything. Some channels are exclusively musical or sports related. Having all these channels running was indeed a change. During Saddam's reign, media and television were state controlled and access to non-state media was impossible. People only saw two or three official government channels, all of which were boring and full of propaganda.

* * *

A few weeks after the war, we all saw on television one of the most amazing expressions of freedom: a spontaneous congregation of a million people or more in the holy city of Karbala for the ceremonies marking the 40th day after Ashura. Only two or three weeks after the collapse of the Iraqi regime, it was time for the ceremonies and hundreds of thousands of people marched to Karbala as is the tradition. What is truly amazing is that in 2003 these enormous marches took place spontaneously, without security measures and without any surveillance. Actually during those days there was not even a government yet. The spontaneity of this event and its success took many people by surprise. It is amazing that this event took place successfully and peacefully. It is another testament to the peaceful nature of Iraqis and the peaceful and respectful interactions between Shia and Sunni Iraqis. If the Shias and Sunnis of Iraq were really apt to have the infamous "civil war" they would have done so during those months when there was no government and no authority. These Ashura and post Ashura events are observed by Shia, but the Sunni Iraqis as well as the non–Muslim Iraqis respected these ceremonies and there was no incident. No attacks happened and no one was hurt. Everyone was happy that they could just participate in this event, something that was banned for many years. That was the first exercise of freedom.

These processions were forbidden for decades during Saddam's time and maybe even before, and people were punished if they revived them or participated in them. So when the procession took place in 2003, that was truly a momentous time and an amazing phenomenon that developed on its own among people who loved to practice their religious ceremonies. This event alone meant so much to Iraqis and to Muslims in general but especially Shia Muslims who have longed for these ceremonies. Now this was truly religious freedom. Religious freedom had been denied for decades. Actually no one dared to think that they had the right to religious freedom. Religion was taboo during the Ba'ath days. But people were even more excited about the then newly emerging political freedom which had never existed for many Iraqis in their lifetime. The ceremonies went normally without violence and everyone was happy that they could participate. It was great. It was amazing.

During those early days, terrorists had not yet entered Iraq. What we typically hear in western and even some Arab media — that Sunni Muslims are the ones who attack the ceremonies — is false. Actually all Iraqis welcome these ceremonies and tolerate them even if they do not believe in them or disagree with them or are critical of them (as are many secular Iraqis). But they would never kill for that. The terrorists who began the killing cycle came from abroad and slowly infiltrated Iraq and of course later found safe haven with Iraqis or non–Iraqis, and that perpetuated the violence.

What most Americans do not know is that Iraqis did not start the so-called "sectarian violence" and the so-called "civil war." When the Ashura ceremonies took place in 2003 only days after the fall of the regime, no violence took place and there was hardly any authority in place. There were no police. The violence took place in later years after many terrorists had entered Iraq and set up their killing machines. These facts must be stated and understood. All sorts of experts today shower us with analysis about the long anticipated "civil war." No one even mentioned this event that I describe here. Prior to 2003, Iraqis were not sectarian people. Unfortunately, today there are many sectarian Iraqis.

These people became that way after being exposed to sectarian violence that was premeditated and that came from abroad but was executed in Iraq after its people had been fed these ideas in recent years.

* * *

Thanks. We Have Democracy!

I was able to come to Iraq because we have a democratic regime. My family and I and hundreds of thousands of people like us were unable to visit Iraq before the regime change. People lived and died in the Diaspora because they could not come to Iraq. A whole new generation of people were born to Iraqi immigrants in many countries, and today some of those young people have still not seen Iraq. There were persecutions and injustice towards us so we could not return under the regime. I am glad things have changed and now I and people like me can go back and help this new democracy succeed and bring a decent life to people in Iraq.

Democracy in Iraq is not a dream come true. Rather, it is something that I and thousands of people worked towards in many ways and for many years. People put their heart and soul into this cause since the 1970s and maybe even earlier. Others gave their blood and their lives into this cause. Thousands of sacrifices in so many ways were given just so that we can have this democracy. We spent years working — in our own small ways — to reach this goal. Since I was a teenager, I spent my time and effort to do what I could to promote human rights in Iraq and to tell the world about the Ba'ath regime. Throughout the years in the U.S., I, my brother and sister and many of our peers volunteered our efforts daily, weekly and monthly to bring the plight of the Iraqi people to America, to the human rights organizations and to the world. We told the world about the abuses and atrocities of the Iraqi regime. This is the dearest thing I have done in my life and is what I am most proud of. Talking about Iraq, the plight of the people there, the crimes of Saddam's regime, was our love and passion and something we did for a long time. We tried to use any opportunity to explain the situation in Iraq.

As a teenager and throughout my twenties, I participated in seminars and events to tell the world about the crimes of Saddam's regime throughout the 1980s. We worked passionately, with a free spirit. We formed organizations, all aimed at exposing the crimes of Saddam. These efforts were largely led and organized by my brother, Ahmad, who had a passion for this cause and a magical ability to inspire the rest of us. And it is from him that my sister and I and the rest of our friends learned to nurture this cause wherever we went. Even more remarkably and more special to me, it is through these activities that I met the man who is now my husband. We volunteered our time together on this cause, and later we got married.

We all volunteered our time day and night, and we used whatever little time and experience we had. We called the media to talk about Saddam's crimes. We organized lectures about human rights abuses in Iraq. Throughout the 1980s, year after year, month after month, week in and week out, we commemorated all the important events that happened in Iraq — which no one even remembers today, and none of those who are at the forefront of the Iraq scene today even care to mention — for example, the 17th of Rajab massacre, the Month of *Saffar* events,[1] and many others. We organized pickets and rallies to commemorate the execution of Mohamed Baqir Alsadr, a prominent Iraqi scholar and thinker. We published several newsletters and posters detailing the accounts of human rights abuses in Iraq. We wrote to the UN, to embassies, to the Arab League, to the White House, and to various senators and congress members. We contacted human rights groups. We voiced what was happening in Iraq. We were screaming out loud about the crimes of Saddam to the world, but no one answered.

As young amateurs venturing into international politics, we learned our first and harshest lesson: that the world community and western countries, all those nice people, do not really move or do anything unless it is in their own interest. And it was not in their interest to do anything against Saddam.

Ironically and sadly the stated policies — then — of many western countries were focused on protecting the "stability of regimes" in the Middle East, and in the U.S. hardly anyone mentioned Iraq in the news or in their conversations. The "stability of regimes," as I understood throughout the years and many heated discussions, has to do with reliable production and delivery of oil from the Middle East. This important goal led to the West's supporting the many dictators of the region, including Saddam. So while we were screaming and striving to talk about human rights abuses and how bad Saddam's regime was, the few "experts" who would once in a while speak about Iraq spoke only in context of Middle East oil and hardly mentioned the atrocities of the Iraqi regime or the fact that the United States was supporting a dictator. This was frustrating to us. We had thought that the democratic West would support us, and we naively thought that they should do the right or moral thing. But actually they did what was right for them, which was to keep the oil flowing smoothly.

We were bewildered by the fact that western countries supported a dictatorship and ignored the human rights abuses in Iraq for the sake of "stability of regimes." How and why did they support Saddam Hussein for nearly three decades? I remember that we followed whatever little bit of news that did get broadcast about Iraq. And over and over we saw the same faces, and those same "experts" ignored the crimes of Saddam and what was happening inside Iraq. They always brushed events off. The name Iraq popped up in the news only once in a while, when there was some major event in the Iran–Iraq war or when the flow of oil was at issue. We were also shocked by how little Americans knew about Iraq and how little they cared.

In reality and in retrospect we were working for something which the "world community" did not support nor care about, and many of them at that time supported the dictator Saddam. As young passionate amateurs we were crushed, bewildered as to why all of these international powers and groups were so oblivious to the plight of the Iraqi people. We did manage to get a few pieces of news published in some local papers, and we got sympathy and moral support from some individuals, and we considered that a success.

I credit and compliment all of us then-young Iraqis who participated in this cause and who brought the facts about Iraq to the world. Our voice was loud and clear in speaking against Saddam's crimes since the 1980s. Our humble efforts kept the fires of freedom burning.

* * *

The world finally acknowledged the crimes of Saddam in 1990 and 1991, during the Kuwait war. Many then started talking about Iraq and

Saddam and how bad his regime was. It became convenient then to use the cruelty of Saddam to mobilize massive world armies against him to liberate Kuwait. All of a sudden it became fashionable to talk about Saddam and expose his crimes, and the experts were ready to do that. And to our surprise and shock, all of a sudden a set of Iraqi "expatriates" popped up out of nowhere. We had not heard of them before.

Some of the expatriate Iraqis whom we saw on television over and over actually only showed up during the events leading to the 1991 Gulf War, and they are main players in the Iraqi political scene today. These personalities who surfaced only in the post–1991 events had no history of opposing Saddam and had not worked in any domain or forum against Saddam. Some were former officers with Saddam. Others were mere businessmen, and still others were complacent or pro–Saddam prior to these events. Yet for some unfortunate reason they were recognized by various governments as the "anti–Saddam expatriates" and were used to support the 1991 call to war.

Further, various new chic organizations were formed and funded by different agencies and governments. And several "foundations" and organizations sprang out here and there, and they all started to speak on behalf of the people of Iraq. Individuals who had never worked for that cause since its inception in the late 1970s and the early 1980s simply showed up at the end to receive money, set up offices in flashy districts in several world capitals, and become self-proclaimed representatives of the Iraqi people. Our sincere longstanding efforts were captured and hijacked by those new fashionable Iraqis. They took over and were recognized, and now many of them are leading figures in the Iraqi political arena.

* * *

I learned about democracy as a young girl who had just come to the United States. I saw it applied in so many areas and events. I saw how people fight for their rights, how they sign petitions and collect signatures and distribute brochures to make their points heard and reach their goals. I saw how elected officials are accountable. Naively, I and many others thought that Iraq would have that democracy too.

To me and to Iraqis like myself who were abroad, a democratic government always meant human rights, freedom to speak, religious freedom, better life for people, justice, and a government that serves its people and that is accountable. This is what I, as an ordinary person, thought it should mean. I do not really know if my definition is even correct according to experts.

A democratic government, I thought, is a means to have a better life for people. It is not a goal by itself. Elections are not a goal. But through elections and through the political process we should have people in government who care about Iraq and who make the well being of its people their priority. These people should work towards fairness in society, safe roads, safe medications, preservation of the environment, and a secure future for our children. In Iraq no one really seems to understand that after elections are over, the elected officials are supposed to roll up their sleeves and get to work on improving people's lives and that with democracy also comes accountability and transparency.

Not the Same "Democracy"

Yes indeed, we now have a democracy. But the Iraqi version of democracy is different from what we all thought democracy was supposed to mean and deliver. The Iraqi democracy does not have the same features and outcomes as democracy elsewhere. The post–2003 era is marked by severe levels of chaos and unaccountability, to say the least. In general, the new democracy is below the expectations of many including myself. I can call it pseudo-democracy or partial democracy or, even more accurately, deformed democracy. Don't get me wrong. Of course I support democracy. Of course it is better now — in spite of all the losses and chaos — and of course we all shall work hard to make it better and make it work.

Pardon me! This is not being harsh. But my whole life is shaped by working for the cause of democracy, all the while assuming that it would bring fairness, justice, better lives for people, punishment for the criminals of the *Ba'ath* regime, and so on. My life is shaped by our activities back in the 1980s — as small as they might have been compared to the sacrifices others made. Indeed it is not only because of my own life's work but because of those very sacrifices that hundreds of thousands of people made, that I can be harsh on this democracy now that it has finally arrived.

II. What Does "Democracy" Mean?

Yes indeed, after all the work and all the sacrifices of Iraqis for four decades, and after the American and international efforts of removing the regime, pardon me — and many Iraqis — for having high hopes and high expectations from this new democracy. Iraqis deserve something good out of this democracy.

Whenever you mention these thoughts you get the counter argument that this is an "infant" or a "baby" or a "young" democracy. It needs time to grow and develop, and it's okay to make mistakes. It takes time to reach perfection or near perfection or even just adequate levels ... and so on. You also hear the argument that all other democracies in the world went through periods of instability and chaos and it is normal to have these things.

I do not agree. I do not agree because the stakes are so high. People's lives and well being are at stake. So, no, it's not okay to make mistakes. This is way too apologist. Why should it be that way? Why do we have to copy everything exactly from others? Why can't we instead benefit from their mistakes and experiences, learn from their turbulent past, and avoid these very ills that other democracies went through? It is almost as if this argument is used to justify the complacency and the apathy and the negligence that is all around in Iraq.

In fact, I propose that we can and we should have even a better democracy than those that are in existence today in other countries, even in western countries. And here is why. As I mentioned, democracy is a big achievement for Iraqis. We can and we should make it work brilliantly because Iraq is a wealthy nation, not only in its natural resources but also in its human resources, and its rich heritage and history. Further, there are still many good values in Iraq toady. As I mentioned before, there are strong family values and ties, there is charity spirit and volunteerism in helping others, and there is the dedication that you can sense in (at least some) people. All of these things can be the basis of a solid and flourishing democracy which can be a unique model in a region struggling to move beyond dictatorships. Our Iraqi democracy can and should be even better than others around.

Nevertheless, it is still democracy, after all. And I support democracy. We do have elections, and we do have free speech and religious freedoms and personal freedoms and no ideologically based detentions — although violence overall increased dramatically because of terrorism. We do have people in the government who would have never been able to participate under the previous regime for a hundred years if not more. There was no hope before. Now we live in different times. I think all Iraqis appreciate these aspects of their newly found democracy.

But Iraqis must also take their newfound democracy with a grain of salt. Along with it came some horrible, almost unbelievable phenomena. For example, violence rose to horrific levels. High officials abused their positions; the astronomically high salaries of the Council of Representatives (COR) members became the talk of the season. Employment is not fair; many qualified regular citizen do not get hired, but family members and relatives of officials get nice positions even when they are unqualified. These are just a few of the problems. As I said before, we can and we should be harsh on this democracy because it must deliver results that are conducive to society's well being. It is not acceptable that after all these sacrifices and efforts of decades, we can't do better than this.

An in-depth look at the problems of this new democracy should begin with 2003 and the years that followed, which were marked first by chaos and bad orders that came with the Coalition Provisional Authority and seem to have stayed. Some of them have evolved to become "laws," and for some Iraqi politicians these are more important than even the constitution. Most of these orders were written in English and were poorly translated to Arabic. Further, they did not arise from an Iraqi environment and were written by people who do not know enough about the complexities of the situation in Iraq. Many of them disregarded the heritage and previous experience and uniqueness of social problems here. These orders quickly became binding without study and without dialogue.

And of course the era then became marked by the emergence of a new phenomenon, terrorism, along with lax security. All of a sudden, soon after 2003, there were alarming numbers of killings, bombings, kidnappings, and explosions. All this was under the umbrella of several elected governments, and worst of all is that these things happened quickly, suddenly, consecutively and simultaneously, so that their effects were severe and shocking. These issues stunned Iraqis and non–Iraqis, inside and outside Iraq. Then came deterioration of already bad services — such as electric power, roads, and so forth — and the phenomenal rise of corruption. The democratic experience which everyone was waiting for was marred right away by these horrible developments.

Explosions became a normal thing that people talk about daily. Bodies are annihilated in the infernos of explosions. Glass shatters near schools and buses. Many people in Iraq dress in black, which is the dress for mourning the dead. There are funeral announcements all over town; every week you hear about someone dying in an explosion. Death in large numbers gradually became a daily event that people got used to hearing about on television. But people whose loved ones perished in those events do not get used to it. They suffer every day. Their lives have now changed forever. There are hundreds of sad stories, enough to comprise an encyclopedia. Iraqis as a society had experienced horrific levels of death and terror at the hands of Saddam's regime, such as the gassing of Halabja, the mass graves, and the killing of entire families because their son or daughter was against the government. However, no one at all, including myself, thought something worse could occur.

Terrorism combined with sectarianism brought new kinds of death, new kinds of fear, and violence that was unheard of. While we who came from abroad are still keen to expose the horrors of the previous regime, many more horrors took place from terrorism, kidnapping, and the scandals of foreign armies during the period around 2004–2007. These terrors surpassed the previous ones. We need a whole new agency just to record atrocities and killings and to investigate each of the terrorist crimes that occurred in Iraq. Events took place that can only be described as the work of organized crime, run by some domestic or foreign groups who were benefiting from this intra–Iraqi violence. People told me that there were areas in Baghdad that no one could go to or leave from. They described how gangs and organized criminals controlled the entry points to main streets of these areas. If those gangs did not like you, or your name or your appearance, they killed you.

These events brought death very close to each person. Dead bodies and scattered corpses became normal sights in some Iraqi towns. Regular people had to act like paramedics, tending to the wounded and dying, and people collecting glass and debris and washing blood off the streets became a daily scene. Deaths of people in large and small numbers became — I hate to say — a normal thing. When we hear of twenty people dying in the Unites States at some event, we get shocked and it becomes important news, and indeed that is how it should be. But, sadly, in Iraq the deaths of many people at once almost lost the power to shock. Bombs, grenades, IEDs, snipers, explosives, became regular words that everyone repeats, even little kids. This is tragic. Nearly every person in Iraq has lost someone in these events. It is a painful reality, and a tax that people paid with the life and blood of their loved ones.

But that's not all. Kidnapping became widespread. This was another new and complex phenomenon. Some people who got kidnapped were killed right away. Others were released on ransom money. These were things we used to hear about only in stories and movies. This had never been witnessed in our recent history. It used to be that if one heard about a crime, it was a big deal. But after 2003, even little children were the targets of kidnapping. Some people stopped sending their kids to school or to kindergarten because of the fear of kidnapping. Others went to school with their kids or stayed at the school gate. Schools sought protection from police or even from families and parents. But in many cases the police were unable to provide the necessary protection because the criminals outperformed them. They had better guns and more sophisticated communication and plans.

Many other events took place that were sad reminders of how much security deteriorated during those few years. Attacks on banks, shops, churches, mosques, and even government offices took place many times. It was evident that these were not random crimes or random terrorist acts. They were systematic, organized, and supported by internal or external groups. No amateur criminals can do such sophisticated attacks on their own.

The well known looting and chaos that took place right after the fall of the regime in 2003 could fill many books and be subject of many investigations. No one knows the whole truth about what happened. Both Iraqis and Americans are to blame for the loss of treasures and documents and heritage and the destruction of libraries. This is one story that remains hidden. I hope one day the truth will be known about it.

To make matters worse, the Iraqi version of democracy is also marked by corruption, nepotism, and incompetent people in high profile positions — as if it were not enough to have to deal with security problems and violence. These terrible phenomena became and still are widespread like a plague. This problem is a consequence of the Iraqi-style democracy.

II. What Does "Democracy" Mean?

Any ignorant, incompetent or even corrupt person can be in a leading position just because he or she has some pull in one major political group. That one person can impose his or her wishes on the whole government. Many ministries, offices, and agencies are contaminated by such incompetence and corruption. The typical Iraqi explanation for this problem is one word: *Muhasasa*. Muhasasa is a product of the Iraqi brand of democracy. It is a quota by which each political group has a share in high profile positions in the government. It is a terrible arrangement because it brings people who oppose each other in one team. It also distributes goods and perks to all the leading political parties.

After 2003 in Iraq, political groups sprang from left and right. There are so many of them today. And although there were — rightfully so — several groups who fought the previous regime for decades, even those produced many sub-groups and sub-factions. These political groups have dominated nearly all aspects of life throughout the years and not just during the elections. You walk into some street and you find it blocked because some political party is using that street for their activities, or they have taken over some property there and used it as their office. You go to some office, and your business cannot be done because the director or the head of the office is from the other political group, and so on.

All these political groups talk in slogans and hardly deliver anything. In fact the whole "political process"—one of those post–2003 terms indeed—produced a lot of jargon and a lot of clutter in terminology. There is so much empty talk from all political groups, those in the government as well as those smaller ones who are not part of the government. We hear talk and terms that no one understands. I hold a doctorate degree from one of the world's top institutions, yet I do not understand what Iraqi politicians and the spokespersons of all these political groups say. For the most part it is mumbo jumbo.

We hear nice words such as *reform, the new Iraq, political process, NGOs, elections, local elections, the constitution, civil society, building institutions, institutional organization, institutional reform, good governance, "electoral rights"* (whatever that means), *regions* (as in dividing Iraq into regions), *disputed territories, civil war,* and so on. People in Iraq hear these terms daily. Everyone repeats these words, and maybe they do not even know what they mean. One person from one political group says one thing, and an hour later another person from the same political group denies what was said and claims that it was the personal opinion of the first speaker and not the official word of this particular party. Iraqi politicians are obsessed with appearing on television. They feel it adds importance to their person. If Iraqi politicians worked as much as they talk on television, there would actually be some results on the ground. People hear this mumbo jumbo daily and hourly on television while their lives pass by with hardship and pain.

Most if not all of these new terms are alien to Iraqis. As someone who grew up in Iraq, I cannot relate to words like "civil war." We never heard of this expression before. This, unfortunately, is a western expression that was implanted and repeated since 1991 and has now become a fact of life. We, in contrast, grew up with pluralism and learned respect for others. This is true for my generation as well as the previous generation. My late father, who came from an elite family in Baghdad, traveled with his friends to northern Iraq and visited the Christian and Izidi communities there *all the way back in 1937.* Dad and his colleagues appreciated the culture and uniqueness of these Iraqis and befriended them. That is civil society; that is tolerance. That is pluralism. We had always been pluralistic. I do not think that we learned about it for the first time it in 2003.

The same goes for the term "disputed territories." That too is an imported term that has now become a part of the political jargon. And when we talk we are supposed to used these "sophisticated" terms. Politicians think it's cool to repeat them. As someone who has lived most of my life in the United States, I never heard the terms "good governance" and "civil society" as much as I hear about them in Iraq — which is daily. It is a dangerous phenomenon indeed that we are drowning in supposedly sophisticated, imported modern terminology, but in reality we are far from these words and they are just being repeated as empty talk.

Today when you talk to regular people in Iraq they make more sense than politicians. They have a clear view about things they need to improve their communities, hospitals and schools. These are basic things, very similar to what we all want for our families and children and ourselves. These are the same things that people in the United States vote on. When presidential candidates in the United States present their ideas and plans for running the country, they use simple terms that we all understand.

II. What Does "Democracy" Mean?

I never heard any congressional candidate or member of congress talk about civil society or good governance.

Regular people seem to be more keen about Iraq than politicians! While politicians repeat too many sophisticated words and use new, attractive, but not-so-meaningful-to-ordinary-people words, ordinary people think about clear, meaningful concepts, and they seem to communicate them better than politicians. They want simple, not complicated, things and things that are essential to their lives. For example, the garbage should be collected, the roads should be paved, the electric power should be on, clean water should be available, and fuel items such as gasoline and kerosene should be reasonably priced.

Perhaps the most overused, misused and over-rated two words in the new Iraq are *training* (*tadreeb*) and *investments* (*istithmar*). These two words have become fashionable. Everyone repeats them. Nearly everyone talks about training employees, counts the number of employees that received the training, and complains that they need more training. I think more training took place in Iraq over the past few years than in the past five decades combined. Similarly everyone talks about investments (*istithmar*) and private sector and free market economy. All of a sudden investors became a hot commodity and all rules have to be bent for them.

Please don't get me wrong: I support training and I support investments. Of course we need them in Iraq. But they should be done correctly. Training should be meaningful and useful. It should have substance. When people complete the training they should have learned something. Similarly, investments should be useful and bring benefit or service to both the end user and the investor. But what is happening in Iraq is that people bring these concepts and apply them in a wrong way or in the wrong place. For example, many over-zealous business people are forcing concepts such as health insurance without having a clue how inapplicable it is in Iraq. And they propagate this concept as the solution to the poor quality of the healthcare services in Iraq. But actually this is hardly the problem. The poor services are not because Iraq does not use the health insurance but because of poor equipment, poor infrastructure, limited number of qualified staff, mismanagement and poor health awareness in society and so on. If these issues are fixed, the health services would be dramatically improved.

* * *

There is an old proverb from the Arab linguist al-Farahidi. It may be translated as follows:

He who knows and knows that he knows, he is wise. Follow him.

He who knows and knows not that he knows, he is asleep. Wake him.

He who knows not and knows that he knows not, he is a child. Teach him.

He who knows not and knows not that he knows not, he is a fool. Avoid him.[2]

To that proverb I would like to add a fifth type of person whom I saw in Iraq: *He who knows not and insists that he knows everything!* Indeed I saw such people. And this is another reason why earlier I said we are headed towards a catastrophe. The new Iraq is marked by high levels of ignorance and ignorance at high levels — and *ignorance compounded by arrogance.*

One would think that with the newfound democracy, there would be more knowledge, more science, more wisdom, more efficiency and more logic. One would think that experts and expertise would be valued and put in the right place to serve. One would hope to see qualified people in the right positions working diligently to solve problems and make life better for people. But no, one rarely sees that! Instead, ignorance and ignorant people are abundant, and they are in top positions. And not just that, they are arrogant too. They think they know it all. And they do not allow those qualified, diligent people to do their work. They put obstacles in front of them. They attack them and make it so impossible for them that the qualified people might quit or get ill.

* * *

I emphasize the problem of arrogant ignorance because knowledge, learning and education are subjects that are dear to me. That is my nature for having been a scientist and an academic for many years, and it is also part of my personality. Knowledge and experience make people humble. But also, I love words, I love books, I love thoughts, I love a good discussion and meaningful conversations. I cherish beautiful words that are said to me; I think about them for hours and even days. I enjoy any beautiful note that is written to me.

II. What Does "Democracy" Mean?

Besides being a personal attribute of mine, my high regard for knowledge and education is also part of the Iraqi character. As I mentioned before, Iraqis in the classical Iraq tended to think highly of education. This is how my parents' generation was, and these are the values that they taught my generation. It used to be that education was a good thing and was highly regarded. There is a residue of these sentiments, as I mentioned before — to the point that some current officials want to add prestige to their CV, so they revert to wrong ways and unethical ways to obtain university degrees. The regard for education explains why there are so many forged diplomas in Iraq. Everyone wants to have academic credentials. They were, and still are to a large degree, a good and prestigious thing to have.

A regard for knowledge is also a big part of Muslim faith. There are numerous references in Muslim belief and tradition about knowledgeable and experienced people. In fact we learn from Islamic teachings that the more knowledgeable people are, the more humble they become. I think that is true, and I have seen hundreds of examples, particularly in the United States. I have met experts and scientists whose knowledge and experience were exhilarating, yet they were so humble. I have met four Nobel Prize laureates, and they too are humble and normal people to be with. So it really shocks and hurts me to see ignorant, arrogant people in charge of important matters in Iraq.

While essential things like reading and writing deteriorate, people have become highly versed in online chatting and video conferences. Somehow they think that these things replace thinking, reading, writing and logic. Of course I do realize that this is in part a global phenomenon and that all over the world younger people's communication and writing skills have gone down because of incorrect use of technology.

I have been continually shocked over the past two years by university graduates who do not know how to write and how to spell properly. Many of them write slang. (In Iraq as well as most Arab countries, slang is only okay for spoken language and is never written. Written Arabic must be formal.) I talk to professors and heads of universities, and they talk to me about nanotechnology and nanoscience and e-learning and virtual libraries while their graduates do not write properly in Arabic, their mother language. Who cares about e-learning and technology when we have not gotten the basics right? Further, while everyone in Iraq talks about electronic this and electronic that, hardly anyone knows anything about important technology issues such as internet security and data security. Everyone uses the internet to transmit important and confidential data without even knowing anything about security. It is indeed a catastrophe. But this is the nature of democracy. People voted. They chose who would represent them and speak on their behalf.

I have registered in my memory and in my soul the good things that used to be in Iraq, things that were established before I was born. The high education standards are manifested not only by the fact that I was able to start university at the age of sixteen when I came to the United States, but also by the great love and reverence that I, and many of my peers, had and still have for our teachers, and how much we love our schools, and how delighted I was when I found out that a colleague who was working in the same office with me was actually my school peer in the late 1970s. It was an amazing moment for both of us. I asked her about our teachers and friends and wanted to know so much about the school news.

* * *

There is much bickering in Iraq. There is bickering in the political process and on an individual level. Everyone you meet has a list of things they want someone to do for them, and they blame everyone else for not being able to meet their demands. There is bickering in offices about who does what. There is bickering, of course, between various political groups and parties. There is even bickering inside families. Everyone criticizes something.

There are way too many conferences in Iraq. Every two or three weeks or so there is some big conference where many officials attend and give speeches. In each of those conferences the attendees conclude that they will take some action to implement the concepts they gathered to discuss. But nearly always, there is no action and there are no results. People in Iraq seem to measure the success of a process by the process itself, not by its results. So many preparations are made for these conferences, such as beautiful flower arrangements, nice chic portfolios and some gifts for the attendees. The attendees (who do not pay registration fees) come and listen to a bunch of lectures, have lunch, and then leave. Although this actually has nothing to do with democracy, this is a common thing in Iraq and throughout the region. These conferences and conventions are ongoing — for the most part, without results — and huge amounts of money are spent on them.

In addition to incompetence and ignorance, lack of morality has also has become normal. People use even vulgar words in English — perhaps with or without knowing what they mean. I was shocked by that. Many Americans who know me do not swear in my presence, and if they do they apologize to me. But high life Iraqis seem to use these words without discretion.

* * *

What is one to do when one sees so much wrong all around? People like me who have courage and guts do something, however small. We point out the wrong and we try to fix it if we can. These are many sincere people who do not approve of the wrong actions or policies that they see. They try to correct them and point out what is wrong. These people are indeed in Iraq. But there are others who are apathetic or opportunists who do not care about the wrong around them or who may be benefiting from the status quo and not want to disturb it. Like many others, I was hoping that the new Iraq would bring many good things along with it in addition to the long awaited freedom. Things that people need on daily basis: cleanliness, road safety, a clean environment, good education, safe buildings, room for creativity, good television programs, health awareness, and much more. It seems that democracy, which is a great and wonderful thing, brought terrible phenomena along with it. Now we see greed, ignorance, cronyism, kissing up to superiors, self-love and arrogance. But that is only one side. On the other side are self-sacrifice, honesty, sincerity, knowledge and expertise. These two antagonistic forces are evident in Iraq, and there is an obvious struggle between them. The problem is there are some people in leading positions who are merely ignorant or self-serving. There are some people who fought the previous regime and might have even been imprisoned and tortured then, but today have changed and become greedy, corrupt individuals.

* * *

Amidst all this bickering and jargon, life passes by. Months and years come and go. Progress is made by good, sincere people and is marred or destroyed by others. People see with dismay that the Iraqi version of democracy does not give them the life they deserve. Many government officials since 2003 have been associated with corruption, crime, money laundering and many other vices such as favoritism, nepotism and lots of unethical conduct. But no one has been brought to justice. No one has been punished or impeached. We have titles of democracy but no substance. Yes, we have elections, and we have members of parliament (Council of Representatives), but they are generally ineffective except for a few. There are indeed some COR members who are sincere and inspirational who truly care. But these are lone voices and not powerful, and they too get swept away when the other big groups make a decision.

And further, amidst all the bickering and conferences and television interviews of political groups, people have hard lives. The electric power problem, roadblocks, traffic, bureaucracy, old rundown unsafe cars, poverty, poor products in the markets — whatever poor quality thing there is out there, it is brought over to Iraq. Children are eating all sorts of imported junk food and junk drinks and even dangerous products. People who smoke in Iraq die quickly. Of course smoking is bad for health. But even the tobacco products that are brought here are probably the worst anywhere. And shopkeepers post the advertisements for tobacco products where everyone sees them, even little kids. Teenagers smoke and unfortunately they think it's cool. Cigarettes are so inexpensive — maybe less than a quarter — that anyone can buy them. It is dismaying to see little kids walking between the cars as they slow down or stop near a traffic light, selling chewing gum or cigarettes or packs of Kleenex just so that they can earn a day's keep. Some of these kids are barefoot and have worn-out clothes. Others are so small that they can't reach the windows of the cars. I saw such kids with my own eyes and in many parts of Iraq: in Baghdad, in several southern cities, and, yes, even up north in Kurdistan. And like many others I ask why the political process has not bettered the lives of these kids, who are the future of Iraq. That is why I think we are headed towards a catastrophe. The success or failure of any political party is indicated by how many such kids are on the streets. And I even saw older ladies (in their fifties) doing the same type of work. The ill effects of these problems will take decades to fix, if they can be fixed at all.

II. WHAT DOES "DEMOCRACY" MEAN?

* * *

I have lived in the West and followed many elections, and I have seen how people prepare petitions and question their representatives in order to achieve their goals. I saw with awe and admiration how regular citizens transform their needs and wishes into propositions and petitions, and how they attend town hall meetings and tell their politicians what they need. And when these politicians do not do as they promised, the people vote them out. When politicians are caught in corruption and lies, they get punished with due process and even impeached for certain violations. These virtues of democracy do not exist in Iraq. Today, all Iraqis are asking is how could it be that nine years after the removal of Saddam, with billions of dollars of both American and Iraqi money spent, most of the daily living problems have not been solved and some service have actually become worse? Why have the successive Iraqi governments not solved these problems? Why have they not made it a priority?

Notwithstanding all that I said, many people, including myself, rightfully defend the new democracy. But we have to correct the wrong that we see and build this new democracy to become better and to really bring out its merits or its benefits. And that's why I am here.

* * *

As a result of everything happening in the new Iraq, some old-fashioned concepts have come back to life. Regrettably, tribalism is well and thriving, and tribal norms rule in some areas. This is a phenomenon that my generation and the one before mine do not even know, because tribalism had diminished during the early part of the previous century. But tribalism is back to life today in Iraq. There is a serious downside to that. Tribal people follow their tribal norms and "laws" or traditions before they concede to civil law, which is the law that governs people's lives.

Tribal "laws" or traditions dictate many things that are in contrast to civil law or go beyond punishment of civil law. One salient example is something doctors in Iraq suffered in recent years, and many of those doctors fled Iraq, fearing tribal law. When a patient dies in surgery or during his time in hospital, the tribe takes vengeance on the attending doctor and wants to punish him as they wish. A similar situation happens

95

in road accidents where someone is injured or killed. The tribal men come over and want to do justice their way.

Tribal sheiks became prominent leaders, and many political groups seek their support and approval because they can deliver votes of their whole clan to that political group. They enhance their power this way, and the tribal elders and young men become like micro-governments, especially in the provinces. This is a dangerous phenomenon, and it was unheard of even in the times of my parents' generation. These traditions had become obsolete a long time ago.

To add insult to injury, the sectarianism that has supposedly "always" been present in Iraq actually arrived, grew and flourished with the new Iraq. Today I am dismayed to hear many people speak primarily in sectarian terms (e.g., Shia—Sunni). It is markedly different from what I am used to in Iraq. It is a new phenomenon. Rarely, if ever, in my previous life in Iraq did I hear sectarian remarks amongst ordinary people, especially young people. There was sectarianism and persecution from the central government and the Ba'ath party, but not amongst ordinary people. I did not know anyone who spoke in sectarian ways. But there are many such people today. It is sad to see that young people today are like that.

For me, I am surprised that any people, whether old or young, have the audacity to speak like that. This phenomenon could be due to the freedom that people are experiencing today as opposed to before, that they have the right to express their feelings and opinions overtly, even zealously. Maybe these people had always been sectarian, or maybe the circumstances today are encouraging them to be so. But the younger people are learning these sentiments. Regrettably, these are the vices of our Iraqi version of democracy. It is not uniting. It is divisive.

In addition, in the name of decentralization and in the name of respecting the special needs of ethnic minorities and localities, new ideologies have begun to arise. In some areas of Iraq, women's status has become limited and governed by male-dominated culture. For example, marriage at a young age is back and has become normal. Also, severe and strict dress codes have become common. On the other hand, and also in the name of freedom, other ideas on the opposite side of the spectrum also have begun to arise — imported social issues such as the call for gay rights and widespread alcohol availability.

II. What Does "Democracy" Mean?

The new Iraq brought me a lot of pain. Days and weeks passed when I felt sad and dismayed at how bad things have become in the name of the new Iraq. I even became ill over it. However, I did not reach the point of despair. Instead, I spent time contemplating one question: Why have things turned out this way?

Perhaps the first problem is the people who are ignorant, who do not know better, but who came into leading positions. These people cannot deliver good results. Then there are others who have personal agendas to reap benefits for themselves or for foreign parties. Those people are abundant, too, and they serve their own interests and could not care less about the public interest. Also, Iraqi politicians have become rusty, aged and overripe. They do not inspire, they do not motivate, they are uncharismatic, and you have to force yourself to listen to them because they do not capture your attention. Perhaps politicians are like that, but certainly leaders should be different. They should be captivating and inspiring.

But there is more to make matters worse. I think many of Iraq's problems would be solved if Iraqis could change one persistent feature that they have. Actually, not only Iraqis have it; it is common in this region. It is called an inferiority complex. The biggest sign of this inferiority complex is that Iraqis — and others in the region in general — seem to think that if you do not speak Arabic or you forgot your Arabic because you were abroad for two or three years, somehow that is a sign of progress. Or if you speak Arabic poorly — even though you have lived in Iraq all your life — you are educated and advanced. What stunned me most is that I met some Iraqis who had attended a college in Iraq where English is the language of instruction — this is normal in Iraq for medicine, engineering and sciences — and during my conversation with them, they seem to say that they have forgotten how to speak and write Arabic!

The other important aspect of this inferiority complex is how they deal with foreigners, westerners in particular. They like them way too much. They pay attention to the foreigners they see and deal with, and they seek their approval at all costs. But there is more: Their body language changes when they are around westerners, and they become apologists about themselves and the way they are. They also become overly critical of Iraq, and they seem to think that whatever foreigners (especially westerners) say is right, even when it is obviously false.

97

I saw such behaviors with my own eyes. In one case, I was in a room with about forty people, all of them Iraqis except for one foreign woman. About 10 of the Iraqis did not speak English, but the one foreign woman was the only one who did not speak Arabic. Yet the day's speaker spoke English because he cared that the foreign woman should understand him. He could not have cared less about the Iraqis who did not speak English. I do not think that he even registered that or gave it a thought for one second. As for the foreign woman, of course I respect her, and many of us in the room spoke English very well and could have easily interpreted for her. But that is how Iraqis are: They care way too much about pleasing foreigners. The speaker cared about the one foreigner and disregarded ten Iraqis.

Here I must relate an experience that happened to a friend, an Iraqi American who worked in Iraq with one of the American agencies. Accompanied by his (blonde) American secretary, he went to meet a senior Iraqi official. Throughout the conversation, the Iraqi official addressed the secretary and ignored the Iraqi American. In the end the official told the secretary that he would like to cooperate and pursue a particular project in specific way. The secretary said she would have to ask her director about that. "Yes, please," said the Iraqi official. "I would like to speak to your director." Then the secretary told him that the director — her Iraqi American boss — was right in front of him. This is typical in Iraq. Iraqi officials and Iraqis in general always think higher of the foreigners. These are just two examples; there are many such stories.

When Iraqis deal with foreign or international institutions they just do what they are told. No one objects or dares to tell the foreigners people that they are wrong. When I ask Iraqis why they are doing what they are doing and how they reached the decision to do their work in that manner, they do not know; they refer to the foreign group members who told them to do it that way. I have explained over and over that this is wrong — that just because some foreign or western people told them to do something in a particular way does not mean it is right, and that we have to examine what anyone tells us and use our knowledge and sound judgment to do things right.

The inferiority complex is also manifested by Iraqis' not accepting whatever Iraqis say, whether they are from inside Iraq or have returned from the Diaspora like myself. Never mind our excellent skills! For example, when some foreign or international organization staff says something, Iraqis accept it right away. Of course I am happy to see international groups come to Iraq and help Iraq in various ways. But I saw only a few of those working seriously to benefit Iraq. Many times what they brought is outdated or does not fit the needs of Iraq, but unfortunately Iraqis (officials in particular) give these people intense attention and broad access to their offices and staff. They even give them access to important data and include them in important meetings. In fact, I know of one senior official who hardly ever has time for his own staff when they need to talk to him, but he meets all the time with some foreign people, who are not highly qualified and many times are delivering only a means of re-inventing the wheel. But not many officials are qualified to know whether what these people are giving them is good or not.

The inferiority complex is also manifested by Iraqis' not accepting themselves and their society as they are and having too much self-criticism. They criticize the way Iraqis look; they do not like their habits, and their skin color, their hair type. They think that everyone should look like foreigners . Even beauty standards in Iraq are set after western looks, as I mentioned before. If you are fair and blonde it means you are beautiful and attractive. The inferiority complex is also manifested by Iraqis' saying that the people of their nation are backwards, cannot progress, and cannot be changed for the better. And it is manifested by their thinking that only certain elite Iraqis should exist and those certain elite should be in touch with the westerners, and then life will be good. I was engaged in such conversations with Iraqis who have condescending views about other Iraqis and think only they and people like them are entitled to have a decent life or even an opinion.

Of course the essence of democracy is that it is representative of everyone in the society. It does not matter if we like people's looks or the way they speak. They are people, and they must be represented.

But why do Iraqis — and Middle Eastern societies — have this inferiority complex? I do not know — this is a question for analytical historians — but I do know it is all over the region, even in non–Arab societies. I have seen many examples, not only in Iraq but in nearby countries, and even in the U.S. among some of my Arab American and Persian American friends.

One Iraqi with whom I worked said to my face, "You Americans!

Why are you here? We are not like you." Yet this very same person also thinks highly of foreigners, and when they come to visit our office he gets very excited. It is bizarre how people react with antagonism to experts and scientists like myself who have taken the bold step of going back to help and rebuild and do important things. The problem is, when there are such thick-minded people who also have an inferiority complex, it is hard to make progress.

In fact it is obvious to me that some people are just waiting for expatriates to leave, and they are also discouraging others from coming back to Iraq. One person persists in asking me how long it will take me to quit and go back to the U.S. "Why haven't you reached that point of exhaustion yet? "Why are you still there? When will you give up?" Someone even had the audacity to tell me and my husband, "It's good you are still here. Some people got assassinated." As if he was sorry that we were still alive!

Further, I faced a similar sentiment, expressed in a slightly different way, from Iraqis and Iraqi Americans in the U.S. who belittled what I was doing. They said that it would not lead to anything good, that I am wasting my life, and that they felt sorry for me.

Some people who are in position to do so seem to be trying to make our daily life harder and harder to entice us to quit. One really has to be made of iron and steel in order to tolerate these tensions and worries. I think that I am generally resilient and have tremendous tenacity and patience, but even I was exhausted after two years of daily (even hourly) tension and physical and mental distress.

I normally do not get affected that easily by what people think, but I must admit that I was disappointed by the bitter and mean attitudes I encountered. It seem people in Iraq and Iraqis in the U.S. do not want to accept that there might be some progress; that I and others are making some difference, albeit small; and that results take time to develop.

Iraq is plagued by this self-hating, inferiority complex phenomenon. Iraq does not appreciate its own, either inside or outside Iraq. It is ironic indeed that Iraqis all over the world are successful and have reached many heights, but in Iraq they are not appreciated. This problem in Iraq is self-inflicted. They do not put the know-how people where they belong. Important positions are given to incompetent people just to please the various political groups and individuals, and of course incompetent people do not work well and do not do things correctly.

II. What Does "Democracy" Mean?

When I went to Korea for an educational program, I met many high profile educational leaders, all of whom were graduates from the best U.S. schools. I was so happy to see all these competent leaders where they belong, and this is what Iraq needs: to put the right people in the right place. But Iraqis do not do that. So much pressure and so much talk took place during the post-election period when we were waiting for the government to be formed (about ten or eleven months), and then regular citizens were disappointed, if not shocked, by the cabinet that was finally announced. None of them were well known technocratic names or high profile professional people or experts. Iraq needed those people so badly in order to make the various sectors of government function properly. Ordinary people could not care less about the political groups. They just wanted a cabinet that was able to run things properly. But the cabinet posts were distributed like perks or prizes just to please various groups. Many people were deeply disappointed.

* * *

Over some two to three years of interaction with various people in work-related matters, I discovered how only a few Iraqis work with zeal and vigil for Iraq, and how most people serve their own agendas first and their job last. Some people, whether they are politicians, businessmen, or just ordinary people in any position — yes, even " poor, helpless" people — enjoy reaping benefits and walking away. There are many examples. Ordinary people seek any opportunity to reap some benefit — for example, more money, or a professional trip abroad even when their skills and qualifications do not match the objectives of the trip. People who are employed and have an income sometimes claim that they are in need of welfare support, and they fake some documents to prove their need. High profile officials abuse their posts and buy excessive furniture at high prices or hire twenty or more of their relatives under some official title while these people do not work. And so on.

I also noted with great dismay how much paper is wasted everyday. I have never seen so much paper used and so many unimportant things printed in many copies, all of which end up wasted and shredded. No one thinks of recycling, saving or reusing paper as people in the U.S. have been doing for decades. Even the use of shredders in Iraq is incorrect. People seem to think that paper shredders are a means to dispose of paper and they use them instead of recycling or just throwing a paper in the trash.

Employees in general do not really work efficiently, and they seem to get tired quickly. Once I was working on some project that involved doing something for three hours. Several of the people with me complained that they were getting ill and fatigued and must find someone to replace them. And these people were much younger than me. I would have thought that they would have more stamina. But at the same time I do give credit to all people who work sincerely, who do not engage in favoritism, who know every detail about their work, and who worked for decades under harsh, underdeveloped conditions but kept going and kept the schools and hospital and factories running.

Iraqis do not conduct office meetings efficiently. Many normal weekly meetings take about two to three hours. This was shocking to me at first, but then I learned it was the norm. People do not get right into the subject of their meeting. First, they have a lot of formalities, and they chat before they start the real subject of the meeting — all during the time set aside for actual work. Many times they digress and talk about other things that were not on their agenda.

* * *

Many foreign development companies and agencies have been in Iraq over the past eight or so years. The more I learned about their work — and I had the opportunity to be directly involved in some of the projects — the more questions they provoked. For example, why don't these groups help Iraqis with important things that are really needed here in Iraq, such as recycling, quality management, internet security, CPR training for all employees and offices, emergency protocols, time management, or professional ethics? All of these things are considered new and are challenges in Iraq. Instead, many projects of international aid organizations are not focused on Iraqi needs. They contain many big words (nearly always poorly translated from English to Arabic) and impressive titles such as — of course — "good governance" and "civil society," but when you read them carefully and analytically there is no substance.

Regrettably, most aid organizations bring ready-made packages from their work in various countries, and many times they are just re-inventing the wheel. I was stunned to see projects about teaching people how to avoid and protect themselves from AIDS when in fact the real threats to their lives are things like malnutrition, cholera, smoking and road accidents.

And foreign aid folks seem to be obsessed with changing Iraqi laws and organizational structures. Wherever I turn, I see people talking about making new laws and new organizational structures. But one can't help noticing that the very same laws and structures worked well and produced good results some forty or fifty years ago. The schools, hospitals, roads, and products of that earlier time were good! But I do not generalize about all foreign aid folks. Some of them are wonderful, dedicated, sincere people who really want to help Iraq.

Elections

I attempted to join parliament (council of representatives, COR) to actually use the political process and be a part of it. Politics is simple for me. I do not hesitate to admit that. I had great motivation and wonderful hope that if we have good, qualified, sincere people in parliament, we would be able to solve many problems. We could do wonderful things ahead. I thought that parliament and being in public service is where you can help people and make things right by being part of the government, holding leaders accountable, and passing laws that bring good changes to people's lives. I thought that if there were intelligent and sincere people in the COR we could achieve results and have progress and prosperity.

It does not work that way. The way it works is, you need to kowtow to some big political group and they will push and support you. It is not dependent on your credentials or virtue or your program to serve people. The reality that exists in Iraq is unlike that. Big, filthy-rich political groups whose money sources are unknown and unregulated acquire people's votes and even lure candidates. They entice people with money or with potential gains: Join me now, they say, and I will give you this or that. People switch their "political parties" when they get a better deal from one or the other. It was weird and not a pleasant experience, brief as it was for me.

Maybe I am politically naive and maybe I do not understand Iraqi politics. I used my own small amount of clean money and my own efforts to market my sincere ideas to the public. I went to the media, I talked on TV a few times, I talked to people as much as I could. I was hoping to inject new blood and fresh ideas into the political process. It is almost as if I was on another wavelength or from another world.

The elections of 2010 and even the ones before had way too many political groups and so many candidates that it was confusing and disorienting. All groups said the same things. All groups claimed that they would deliver good things, that they were not sectarian, that they loved all Iraqis. There was so much repetition. One heard the same things over and over. There was really no one in any group or party who truly captured the souls and hearts of people. There was no one in whose voice people heard their wishes and no one in whose vision people saw their dreams and the future of their children. There was no one who inspired and moved people and made them rise above petty things. And in the end, most people voted based on their ethnic or sectarian identities and not on how good the candidates or the programs were. It became apparent during and after the 2010 elections that parliament is not really the prestigious place I thought it to be where high caliber people work hard to make things better.

In the elections many good individual names were in various political groups. But these good people got swept away and their influence was diluted in the big groups. Those who made it to the COR were tamed to follow the group, or they resigned because they could not be tamed. It is a loss to Iraq that such intelligent, sincere people, after having made it to COR, found it necessary to not say their true opinion or to quit because they were not heard and their input was not taken seriously.

Today the Iraqi parliament is plagued by political bullying, bickering, point-scoring and blackmail. All these features are evident in the Iraqi parliament while the most important feature — well, I thought it was — is not present at all, and that is loving public service and wanting to help your people. It seems that all that COR does is bicker. Of course there are some in parliament who care about public service, but they are few and I wish them the best.

* * *

II. What Does "Democracy" Mean?

One might argue that bickering and partisan politics also exist in other countries and are part of the nature of these elected bodies. Experts and some parliamentarians would say that this is how politics is and how democracies are. Of course there is always bickering among competing political groups all over the world, but the parliaments and officials of these other countries *produce results and the lives of regular people are reasonably good.* They have basic services, roads, and so forth. They do not live the harsh lives that Iraqis do.

But more importantly, why do we have to copy only the bickering and fighting from other countries? Why don't we copy the good things, too, and even do better? Why can't we improve this new democratic experience elections and representation that we just tasted for the first time? And if our democracy is young, as the argument goes, then why can't this very young and beautiful democracy also be fresh and free from features of ailing and mature democracies like bickering and arguing? Why do we always get the worst of everything?

The major political players do not want independent thinkers among them. Quite the contrary: They want those very same smart, good people to support whatever they do in order to boost it and give it credit. Political groups want high caliber and high profile persons joining and supporting them, to be a credit to the political group.

In fact I talked over the months with a few current and former members of the council of representatives, and they all say the same thing. Their party or coalition leaders command them to vote one way or another and they must follow the instruction of their group. There is not room in that arena for intelligent debate and coherent analysis of issues.

Of course I know there are interest groups and political moves in other established democracies, but I also have listened to debate, reason, scientific evidence and testimonies from people who are affected by laws and products. There is good debate and good information in other parliaments and congresses of other democracies. Not just the bickering and manipulating.

Notwithstanding all of the above, people in Iraq were so eager for democracy that they participated in the political process. These nice-sounding things like elections and voting and so on resonated well with them, especially because they see how these very same things have been employed in many countries and led to good results. Therefore, people participated in spite of the difficulties such as security issues, poverty and disability.

But then reality hit. As the saying goes: What goes around comes around. Scandals become apparent sooner or later. And those same chic politicians do not follow important values such as accountability. They do not fight corruption, and they engage in favoritism. People participated wholeheartedly and did what they were supposed to do, but the reality is, people's lives have not improved as a result of the elections. Sure, it is nice to have elections; it gives people the feeling that they control their destiny and that they are responsible for their lives. But if only these elections were real and meaningful! It is good to elect someone and give him a legal and moral legitimacy. But once he comes to power, he does not serve his constituency; he indulges in money and desires, or he serves the interests of foreign entities. Elections should lead to meaningful results. Elections are not just a nice decoration.

And in order to please all these groups who ran the show during the elections, a government was formed from all the various groups The so-called Partners' Government or Government of Partnership means all the big and small groups must have a share in the government and all its agencies. So there is no opposition in the COR because they are all in the government. No accountability. All recent governments of the past few years have had key people — such as ministers, deputy ministers and others — from various groups according to a quota. Many such people were not only unqualified but themselves made matters worse by hiring more unqualified people based on nepotism and favoritism. Those people do not know what they are doing, so they ended up with various disasters and blunders, not to mention they wasted huge amounts of money and reaped enormous personal benefits. As a result of all these political factors, corruption, ignorance, and incompetence began to reign and have become like a monster today.

* * *

I have reflected a lot about why people in high ranking positions have so much apathy, why they are so negligent and self-serving. Why don't they care about their constituents? Why do they only care about their perks? I think it all comes down to the same human vices that exist everywhere in all societies. Some people are refined because of their upbringing and values and because they do live and practice their values. Others refine themselves with high discipline and fear of God.

It all comes down to greed, jealousy, being overly proud about one's self and one's accomplishments, and also flat-out arrogance. Persons who have not refined themselves either by discipline or by their own background, upbringing and experience are the ones who, when given the opportunity, will abuse their power. They will abuse and misuse their positions by accumulating more money, more women or more power. And they think these things bring them prestige and that they can control people.

This scenario is not unique to Iraq. All over the world and throughout history these behaviors have destroyed the very persons who engage in them. How many times have we seen and heard of bigshot CEOs, presidential candidates, and celebrities who get into financial and sexual scandals? In the end, what goes around comes around.

Actually this debate is ongoing in Iraq. I have been with some ordinary middle class people and they all talk about the conduct, the scandals and the abuse of power of politicians. Whenever this topic is brought up, people have theories about why "leaders" and politicians behave that way. What do they think? Do they think they will never be caught? Have they no shame? And usually one hears two answers: One is that these greedy people are all from low class background. They had little when they were growing up, and that's why they indulge on money and women when they have a chance. The other theory is that power corrupts and that even good people, people who one would never imagine would do wrong, actually do wrong when they are in powerful positions.

Certainly power corrupts some people, but not all people. So what makes some people immune from being corrupted when they have power? Iraqis think they have made theories about this subject. They present reasons that go back to classism issue I described earlier. They would say: "Who were those people before? They were nobody before." But this is racist and classist.

Regardless of the reasons, politicians and high profile people are busy with their fun; they have no time and energy to care about people who truly deserve their attention. People who gave up important things

107

from their lives. People who are sons and daughters of families who were harmed by the previous regime and whose lives were shattered.

* * *

But amidst all those disappointments, there are also amazing, inspiring efforts. There are dedicated Iraqis — even among politicians — as well as Iraqi expatriates doing wonderful things: helping, building, never tiring. Those are the heroes. They work hard, they are relentless, they keep giving and pouring out their time and their effort. They work hard, they do not bicker and complain, they know how hard it is to get things done. Seeing such people inspires me too and makes me keep going. I love those people and I salute them. They do it because they are responsible, love to help others, and care about the future of the children of Iraq.

NOTES

1. Important events in Iraq where the Ba'ath government crushed opposition.

2. Common translation of the Arabic proverb by al-Farahidi.

CHAPTER III

The Blueprint

Romance on the Border

The most romantic moment in my life took place in the rugged terrain at the Iraq-Kuwait border where I had a rendezvous with my husband at 10:00 on a cold November morning in 2003. This was just a few months after the war, and I was visiting Iraq for the first time, for just a few days. My husband had already gone to Iraq before me and met with his family, most of whom he had not seen for three decades. Knowing how adventurous and high spirited I am, he told me to come to Iraq to see things first hand and more importantly to meet most of his family and extended family for the first time. I had met some of my in-laws who were able to travel outside of Iraq during the previous decades, but most of them I did not meet until 2003. He told me to fly to Kuwait City and then come to the border region; he would meet me at the border. He thought that if anyone could do this venture it had to be me. I took the offer, flew to Kuwait, and arranged with kind friends there to take me to the border the next day.

During that time in late 2003, there were no commercial passenger flights to any city in Iraq, not yet. People who came by planes to Iraq used some special chartered planes that were related to the United States or the UN. Therefore I flew to Kuwait City and drove to the border and had to continue across the Iraq-Kuwait border. I was riding with our kind friends from Kuwait. It was cold but sunny that day. We left Kuwait City and reached the border. The terrain became bumpy and muddy, and the roadway was busy with trucks, military vehicles and a few lone cars.

I talked to my husband, who had a special satellite phone. To add to the complexity of things, there were no cell phones in Iraq at that time. The satellite phone was the kind you could just use from anywhere on earth. It is not like the cell phone where you must sign up with a provider company. The satellite phone was the most reliable form of communication because even the land phone lines became dysfunctional during the war.

My husband told me that he was already there waiting for me on the other side of the border. That was my last contact with him, because my mobile phone which I had brought with me did not pick up the signal further in the area. My friends dropped me at the last point in Kuwait as they were not allowed to go any further. They waited for me to pass the border. We decided that I would ride that small distance with one of the commercial cars that crossed the border. I rode with a total stranger.

The distance we had to travel was very small — less than one kilometer — but I was out of touch with anyone. And the short ride seemed to be taking a long time, perhaps because of all the anxiety I felt. I was alone in that car. I did not even know the driver. There were no women in the whole border area. I thought maybe I was going to be harmed or kidnapped or my passport or money confiscated or stolen. All sorts of uneasy thoughts came to my mind. That was one intensely anxious twenty minutes in my life. To add to the fear and anxiety I was going through, there were no signs on the road. It was a trip to the unknown, to the Iraq which I had left more than twenty years earlier. More importantly, it was a part of Iraq that I had not seen before. We would be driving through the southern region of Iraq, and I had lived in Baghdad all along when I was a child.

After the brief but intense anticipation during the short ride which separated us, the car entered the Iraqi side. I was immediately elated to see my husband waiting for me — literally — in Iraq. I know it sounds crazy to depict romance at a rugged border zone during a war. Well, we had never ever seen each other *in Iraq*. All of our life together had been in the United States. So to meet in Iraq, at the border region and amidst military vehicles, was a new type of romance with a dramatic flavor. My husband had arrived in Iraq a few weeks earlier, after he had left it twenty-six years before, in the mid–1970s. At that time my husband and

I had not seen each other for some four months, and the rendezvous in Iraq was a turning point for both of us. Not only was this our first time together in Iraq, it was my first time setting foot in Iraq after twenty-three years away and the first time I had met most of my in-laws. It was a very special moment in my life.

There were a few other people waiting for their family members or visitors. The place where people waited was just a point on the ground near the Iraqi immigration booth. But there was no place for passengers and relatives to meet. People simply met in the wide open space. There were no cabins and no buildings, really nowhere to sit and wait. People either waited in the car or out on the road.

I was happy for us to be united after not really a very long separation but a highly dramatic one. I waved at him and was delighted when he saw me. It was like once again meeting for the first time. Even for a strong person like myself, that trip was a tense and dramatic time indeed.

When it was time for me to leave after a few days, I did the reverse trip. This time we drove towards the border in southern Iraq and there were no cars. I crossed the border walking in the mud with my luggage. Our friends from Kuwait waited for me at the other side.

I have been through many other dramatic moments in my life like crossing the border. I have been put in hard circumstances many times and made it out in one piece. I grew up away from my family during my critical teenage years and was independent and responsible at an early age. This has made me tough and resilient, I think, and many people who know me would agree. I started college at the age of sixteen. I lived away from my parents at the age of fifteen. I learned to budget my money and be responsible since then. I worked two jobs at some point in my life. I went through some health issues in my early twenties. I have done lots of traveling and many other things. All of these things were challenging, even amazing, and because of all those broad experiences I have always thought of myself as rather strong.

I also remember well the day I went to the hospital in London with my parents when my dad had a stroke around midnight in the cold. I did not know where I was in London. I had just arrived two days earlier, and I had no sense of where we were. I went with the ambulance and then had to go back to the house, as I had left door unlocked amidst the panic. I was nineteen years old.

All these tense moments developed my character and made me strong and resilient, and of course these tough moments helped me survive in Iraq. But nothing, nothing prepared me for the feelings I had as I approached our home in the Almansour district in Baghdad in 2011.

Visit to Almansour

It was April 14, 2011. A dear friend took me to where our house was. She was friends with my older sister from school. She lived nearby in the same area and she knew our house well. It was my first outing to the Almansour district where I grew up. It was a memorable outing for me. First, I am glad that Almansour, which was highly posh in the 1970s, is regaining its posh stance and is still considered *the* posh place to go to. It still has — relatively, and considering the circumstances it went through — elegant, stylish people and some elegant shops. Almansour district, like several other areas in Baghdad, suffered a lot during the years of instability; most people say that from 2006 until 2009 things were really bad. During that period, security all over Baghdad declined very markedly, but the Almansour area deteriorated badly and became a haven for terrorists and gangs. After 2009, however, security improved, and Almansour also recovered and regained its liveliness. So when I went in April 2011, it was reasonably pleasant.

The main road, named "14 Ramadan," that led to the area of our house did not look the same to me. It looked smaller, narrower, shorter and more crowded. Amazingly, however, I knew my way very well there. My heart was racing. I was overwhelmed. I felt strange, anxious, excited and nostalgic. I felt intense but confused emotions as I looked left and right down the main road, orienting myself. I was happy to know my way around in my old neighborhood. This was the very road I used to walk on with my sisters and cousins as we used to go buy ice cream. It felt like I had been asleep and just woken up. The area had changed, and there were many more shops and offices crammed together there. It used to have more open space before.

Then we arrived at the small side road leading to our house. We had to stop the car and walk the rest of the distance because a military checkpoint and barricades prevented cars from passing through. (Although this is outside the IZ, there are many checkpoints and barricades in Baghdad.) We took those few steps from the main road to where our house was. I was drowning in my thoughts and imagination.

I wanted to stop at every step and soak myself in all that was around me. I wanted to gaze at the scene, to touch the ground, to take note of the background noise, to listen to birds and to the chatter of people as they walked about. I wanted to sit there at the doorstep of the house for hours, to feel the same sun in the same place years later. I wanted to inhale and inhale the air. I wanted to walk barefoot on the patio and in the garden. I wanted to run my palms along the rugged rocks of that stunning, tall wall layered with unusually shaped and sandy-colored stones. I wanted to lie on the grass, then sit under the grapevine, I wanted to stand for hours in the calming shade of that walkway around the house with its dusty-purple ground, remembering my solo walks there when I used to recite my homework, as well as my walks with Dad as he sprinkled the trees with water in the summer evenings. I wanted to run the water in the garden and splash it around me as we did decades ago. I wanted to turn on the muddy water faucet (a special faucet used to irrigate the gardens in Iraq, found only outside homes, where it turns on with more power and vigor than the normal water) in the canal that runs along this pathway, and listen to the intense sounds of the gushing water as it filled the canal and irrigated the bushes and trees. I wanted to go to the other patio near the garden which had the semi-oval little pool with its turquoise and white ceramics and maybe fill it with water and wet my feet there. I wanted to stand at the high porch that overlooked the garden — which I loved very much — and remember our sunny weekends when a few times we had breakfast there. I wanted to touch a door knob, *any* door knob, to look through the glass of a window and to open the doors and go inside.

But I got to do none of that.

* * *

I am no entrepreneur. I do not know much about business. I do not know much about making money or investing money. I do not strive to have lots of money. Having money does not bring me pleasure; I merely use it to be comfortable in my life. I like to have just enough money in order to live comfortably and without economic hardship. I have worked hard all my adult life to earn whatever money I earned. No one handed me large sums. Money is good to have but is not the most important thing to have. I have donated my own money to help various people whenever I could. I have nothing against making money, nor against people who like to acquire it or invest it.

However, when my some of my siblings decided to demolish our house, and when they actually executed their decision so quickly — before I had a chance to go see the house — just for the possibility of yielding some profit when sold as a vacant lot as someone had advised them, that was beyond what I could take. Yes! I am talking about the very same house that I was fantasizing about, the very same house that I was aching just to see and touch. Not only did I not have enough time to digest the bizarre idea of demolishing the house and to find reason in it, the demolition was executed so quickly and suddenly that I was helpless to stop it or just delay it a few months until I could go there. I attempted to stop this bizarre demolition, but I was labeled as being too attached to bricks and stones, told that I was emotional and sentimental and not practical, told that I needed to get real.

When I went to Almansour as I explained above, I knew the house had been demolished. I had heard about it from my siblings a few weeks before, and I was very sad when I heard about it, but it is different when you see it.

Words fail me, and I am someone who loves words. Sentences crumble in front of me as I attempt to relate what I felt when I arrived there. Shock, vacuum, numbness, sadness, nostalgia, sorrow — all these are powerless words and cannot convey what I felt when I saw the empty lot of what had been our home before. At first, seeing the huge lot, I was disoriented; I even felt dizzy, as though standing on the edge of a cliff. The sun was too bright in the vacant lot. I felt like I just had a sharp jolt or a cold slap, not on the face, but on my heart and on my soul.

Although the three small streets at the location were the same as I knew them from before, the big vacant lot was frightening. It stunned me. It struck me. I tried to maintain my composure and looked around to orient myself, and I found a couple of landmarks. Most of the flowers and trees were long gone — even long before the demolition, because the house had not been cared for. But the palm tree got me my sense of direction back. How happy I was to see it in the same place!

When I was a child it had been a young palm tree, standing in the corner of the garden. It was surrounded by smaller bushes of flowers. It stood there like a bride amidst all the people attending to her. The palm tree was healthy and luscious then, a bit taller than me. I was surprised by how tall and how old it had become. Very tall, maybe seven or eight meters high, but it was ailing and looked ill. It was dry and looked nothing like what I might have expected. In fact, I did not like the looks of the old, ailing palm trees in homes even when I was a kid. They made the homes feel old, and they kind of gave me the creeps. And now there was nothing there keeping the palm tree company except dry dirt, dead bushes and the fence that still stood there.

My other landmark was the structure over which the grapevine grew. It was still there, but of course it too was barren. Only the metal parts were left. It used to have nice gentle shades and was full of grapes when in season — but not anymore.

* * *

I would have thought that the many intense experiences of my life had prepared me for anything, but I was not prepared for walking into our home thirty-one years later and finding it a wreck, dissolute, abandoned, run down, dry, barren, no flowers, no trees, no life. I was dismayed, shocked, and immensely saddened by what I saw. It was nothing like what I knew to be a lovely home with trees, flowers, laughter, friends, and yes, even standoffs with the previous regime.

Even though the house was not there, sensations of melancholy overwhelmed me as I thought of the structure that should have been there and imagined that I was looking through the glass into the living room. Every nerve in my body was electrified. The time, the location, the sun, all evoked my memories and took them out of their stores. They got tossed at me, they struck me, and they bombarded my heart and my soul.

I remembered, for a second, the terror of that day — December 15, 1973 — when my dad did not come home. I remembered how I stood in the mid-house patio garden, fearing and worrying. This day is imprinted on my soul. I wish I could say to Mom and Dad how afraid and helpless I was on that day. Pain does not go away; it only gets buried with time. And when it is awakened, it brings tears and sadness like an erupting volcano.

Actually, because there were some people with me — the friend and the driver who were kind enough to take me there, as well as several guards and workers who had occupied the lot for their use — I hid my feelings and controlled my emotions. But I was not all night.

I do know the house's layout very well, like a map I memorized. If I had the chance and if the lot had not been used by guards of some bigshot military person nearby, I would have sat there for hours enjoying my memories and at least imagining the scent of the trees and the colors of the flowers. I would have walked where the long pathway once ran around the house, I would have looked at the remains of the doors and the walls and maybe would have found a fingerprint from Mom and Dad, or maybe I would have found, among the bricks and the debris, a letter, a bracelet, a pen, any small memento from home. I would have, maybe, saved a brick or collected a few blue ceramics. I would have at least taken a thousand pictures of a thousand corners and dear spots that I used to walk and sit in. And I would have been happy even just to get my hand in the rubble and dig my way through it to find a secret written prayer that was hidden in the walls!

A long time ago, when I was a child and I was afraid during all the bad events that happened to my family in the seventies, my Mom tried to reassure me, telling me she was sure we were safe in our home. She told me that when the house was being built in the mid–1960s, she and Dad used to come periodically to check on the building progress. (Iraqi homes are typically custom built and normally you would hire a contractor, who would do the work over a period of several months or a year.) And during her visits to the house while it was under construction, Mom buried a written prayer in the walls of the house. That was why she was sure we were protected within our house. My mom had strong faith.

I know about this prayer that was buried in the walls. I would have loved to find it amidst the rubble. I would have cherished it and held it close to my heart. I would have read it over and over. But that piece of paper, too, was probably lost amidst the debris.

For security reasons, I could not stay long in the lot. Further, the entourage of the military person was sort of camped there, making it a home base.[1] That was the only visit I made.

Because of the demolition, I am missing a whole lot more words and feelings that would have been stirred in my soul and would have arisen and been a part of my life had I just seen that house once. I call the demolition a mistake and try to let it go. But no one knew how much I was really hurting, and how speechless and overcome I was, when several well meaning friends asked me, "Why did you demolish the house?"

I heard about the house having just been demolished from someone who actually saw it and told me about it soon after, and then, after a few weeks, I went to see the place. Actually, just hearing about it was hard too. A weird sensation overtook me, like the feeling you have when you are nauseated, plus some confusion. But I ached more when I actually saw it. And it hurt me further to see the barren land used as a military campground. Strange men wandered on my property as if it were free for all.

I am rarely speechless. Anyone who knows me would probably agree that I normally have an answer for most questions and that I am never short of words to say what I want to say — if I know what I want to say. But when friends asked me why the house was demolished, I did not know what to say. Once I was talking to someone I had just met and learned that he was a close friend of my brothers and that he practically grew up at our house. He told me how much he loved the time he spent there, and he asked me whether I had gone there yet and what I felt. I answered that the house had been demolished. He too was stunned and asked me why, and that was when words failed me.

Mom and Dad built that home and gave us a good life in it. I am grateful to them for having provided such a wonderful home, and I wish they could hear my gratitude and appreciation. They built that home with much effort, and they poured their hard-earned money into making it nice for us. How much each brick meant to them, and how each corner was designed with softness and care! How beautiful it was inside and outside, and how stimulating to the mind and soul it was! The sun, the space, the sounds of water in the canals, the trees, the flowers, the decorations, the ornaments, the love and care. This beautiful, enriching environment gave us the freedom to live, to think, to relax, to be creative and to play. I am grateful to Mom and Dad, and I am sorry that the place is no more. But I am glad to have a beautiful memory of it and to have documented some of it. I am rich and lucky because I have memories, and I will strive to keep them, protect them, and express them in words.

Me (left), Dad and my sister Abtihal at the small gate of our house in Almansour during the Eid Alfitr religous holiday a few months after Dad's release from prison.

III. The Blueprint

During that same visit to the neighborhood, I walked into the flower shop that I used to go to. It is just a few steps from the location of our house. I could not believe the pretty flowers and chic shop in the Almansour district had survived all these years of agony and dearth. I talked to the store manager and told him that I used to come over to this very store and buy stunning bouquets. The shop was in the same place and still looked nice and elegant.

* * *

I am no engineer and no designer. I do not like reading maps, and I do not appreciate house plans and layouts. I guess I am not that visual, and I always prefer verbal descriptions of things over diagrams. Still, when I got my hands on a blueprint among some family documents that were delivered to me by my cousin — as my aunt had saved them for us over the years — and when I examined the blueprint and realized it was indeed the blueprint of the house, it was both a delight and a consolation. It was the blueprint of the house and the designs and drawings that the engineer had prepared before building the house. It is from the early 1960s, before I was born. My family had moved to the house just several months before I was born.

I held the blueprint, I opened it, and I looked at the various parts of map. I loved its dark blue color and the cute descriptive words — written even before I was born — "children's room." The patio overlooking the garden, which I loved and I miss so much, was there too. I saw the garden or patio in the middle of the house. It was sensationally called "the lit area" (in Arabic *Mnawara*).

The blueprint healed my wounds. It filled the vacuum that bothered me, and it re-oriented me. I feel anchored to the ground. I shall keep it as a dear reminder of the house. I am going to frame it and display it. It helps my memory, so as I age, it will help me remember and reflect.

* * *

To my delight, among the aforementioned family mementos and documents, I also found my school autograph book, with its very same pretty colorful pages and its gritty texture. This is a small notebook that typically girls kept for years. Normally we would pass it to our teachers and elders such as aunts or uncles or older relatives. They would write wishes and words of wisdom to us kids. I was so happy when I found this notebook. I loved touching it and feeling its then fancy textured paper. I loved holding it and turning the pages to find the sweet words of my teachers and my elders. I found lovely comments written in the early and mid–1970s. I read with pleasure what my primary and secondary school teachers had written to me, encouraging me, admiring me, wishing me success and appreciating my calmness and my being a good pupil. I am so lucky to have found this notebook after missing it for so many years. I cherish this notebook, its pages and its words. I wish my teachers — I think they might be still around, albeit old — could know that I still have this autograph book and how much I love and appreciate their words and sweet wishes to me.

The autograph book is not only a treasure for me but also a testimony about teachers. When I give speeches or talk to my relatives and colleagues, I always say that we were raised with high values of loving and respecting our teachers. We looked up to them and thought highly of them. We feared and revered our teachers. We wanted their approval. We admired them. We wanted to be like them. We carefully looked at their clothes and we liked to emulate them. We even had a day to celebrate teachers, called teacher's day. We honored our teachers on that day, and we prepared beautiful flowers to give them. These are the values I know and I grew up with. I would be so delighted to meet any of my teachers today to thank them for inspiring me and teaching me. And perhaps the worst thing Saddam's regime did was destroy teachers.

How did that happen? During Saddam's rule, the salaries of all employees of public agencies became very low because of the inflation in the currency that followed the Gulf War of 1991. The UN economic sanctions that followed aggravated this situation and created a layer of poverty unheard of before in Iraq. This was the main cause for the erosion and the deterioration of the teaching profession, although there are other important reasons such as the regime's policy of punishing all professors and professionals who did not join the Ba'ath party.

Because of the severe economic hardship, teachers became very poor. The pupils whose parents had money manipulated teachers into making them pass or letting them skip class in return for material favors. Regrettably, many teachers became slaves to the rich, high profile families of the pupils. Professional ethics did not reign, but economic need. Although there were good teachers who did not engage in such behaviors, many did in order to survive.

This phenomenon also affected universities. And today there are trains of university graduates and holders of university degrees who cannot write or speak properly. The effects of devastation of the teaching profession are so severe that a whole generation of people today in their twenties, and some even in their early thirties, do not speak or write Arabic — their mother tongue — properly. They use slang in their writing, they cannot spell properly (by the way, Arabic spelling is much easier than English; most words are written as they are pronounced, so it should not be that hard to write correctly). And although Arabic grammar is indeed very hard, it was taught very well when I was a child, to the point that today, I — who lived abroad in English-speaking countries most of my life — actually know Arabic grammar and writing better than most people I met in Iraq. This is shocking and disheartening, and there are no signs that it is getting better yet. The wrecking of the language tops the entire devastation of the previous regime. This is the thing that hurt me most in Iraq: that there are people who do not speak or write properly. I keep repeating it here in this book and wherever I go because it really shocked me. I am stunned and worried about this, and saddened to the point that I myself— I who have been a scientist and researcher, I who have held high level positions — am willing to quit what I am doing and work as a primary school teacher just to save the future that I see is slipping away. It is sad, and even alarming, that in this day and age the new Iraq is not successful in something as basic as teaching the native language of the country.

Language defines a people and defines the person. Language is beauty; it reflects coherent thinking and a clear mind. Some people do not have any love nor pride in using their own mother language correctly and beautifully. Language is character; it is the key to culture. When language is marred, all of these things are marred.

There is a common misconception among Iraqis — and actually this has been around a long time, not just since recently — that those who study engineering and science do not need to know Arabic. They feel that somehow because their fields are technical in nature, learning proper language is not that important to them. They are wrong, of course. And that misconception contributed to this phenomenon. I have tried and tried to explain to many people that in the United States, people in all fields of study must learn the skills of critical reading and analytical writing. I tell people how serious these subjects are in high school and in university and that no one graduates from university if they do not master these skills. In fact, when I was an undergraduate student, writing courses were among the first mandatory classes that I took.

We are headed towards a gloomy, dark tunnel as these twenty- and thirty-year-olds of today become the leaders and educators and doctors who will guide the next generation. Sadly, they do not have much to give. I met a few people who graduated from Iraqi universities in the 1980s, and there is a significant difference between them and the younger generation who have graduated since the late 1990s. The latter group is very weak in their credentials. It is not their fault; the system collapsed, and this weakness is the result. There are some old professors who studied abroad in the 1960s and 1970s; those people are well qualified, but their knowledge has become old, although they have sound background and skills. I met a few people who graduated in the 1970s, and they too have good, sound knowledge and a strong skill base. Some of them are employees in various ministries. The lower ranking staff in the ministries know their work, and they do it well. They just need modern tools and constant revision.

I do not agree that the entire structure of Iraqi organizations needs to be changed. In Iraq today there is a fashionable notion that all that existed for decades is not good enough and that the problem is in the structure of things. I do not agree. I always pose this question that no one can answer: Why is it that the same organizational structure of the ministries and agencies previously produced good results in areas such as education, health care, agriculture or small industries, but now we cannot do any of these things like our predecessors did?

Here too I pay tribute to my parents' generation. Benefits from what they accomplished in their time are still in Iraq. They did things so well that society still benefits today from their efforts. I met one high official whom my father had taught in university. And I met some gracious fine ladies who were my mother's students in secondary and high school.

In fact, I met several friends of my parents. A wonderful gentleman who knew my parents told me beautiful things about them. I further met an old family friend who knew my mom and dad and even my aunts and uncles. He was a neighbor of my family long before I was born. He know many stories about the family. He put me in touch with his daughter. She is in the U.S., and I plan to meet her. I also met a friend of my brothers who knew my parents very well and mentioned them in such sweet words. He said that my parents were parents not just to their own children but also to him and the other young men — the group of my brothers' friends, including himself. They used to converse with my dad about his experience living abroad and having education in the United Kingdom and what their aspirations were at that time. This man loved our house as much as I did. He is older than me by some twelve or thirteen years. He said he had seen me when I was a little kid, five years old or so. This was so cute and sweet. How ironic it is to have all these delightful stories from the past.

* * *

Special wrapping paper also reminds me of my teachers and my school. The colors of that particular glossy wrapping paper intensely evoked my memory from first grade and touched my heart. Red and dark green, glossy, soft wrapping paper. I have not seen such paper in the United States. It is like craft paper, but the colors and texture are unique. I remember them very well from first grade as the teacher asked us to wrap our notebooks with different colors of that particular paper. Shiny, soft red and dark green paper is so special to me that I bought a set and I look at it often. Call me emotional; call me whatever you want. To actually experience these memory jolts is beyond what words can describe. It is like having an earthquake in your mind and in your soul. It is amazing.

* * *

Righteousness

I am looking at a treasure of letters and documents from the past. Among them were some old photographs, documents pertaining to our house, and the Kubba family tree, a long, rolled, handmade document whose parts are pasted together from smaller sheets of paper. I remember this delicate document well. Dad showed it to me and my sisters when we were kids. I remember that he pointed out our names and his name on the family tree.

I even found the marriage certificate of my great-grandfather in this treasure of documents, from all the way back in the late 1800s. That sheet of paper was fragile and had turned yellow. More interestingly, it was written in the old Turkish language, as Iraq was part of the Ottoman Empire then. The old Turkish language used Arabic characters, so I could read some of it.

Further, many of those documents pertained to Dad, his work, his prison ordeal and his professional achievements. There were records of the incident of the broken desk at work. Immediately those documents captured my attention because there were several of them. I examined them carefully: In that incident in 1968, shortly after the Ba'athists took power, Dad had gone on an official business trip. When he came back and reported to work, he found his office in shambles. His desk had been broken into, and some documents were missing. Dad was shocked, angry, and concerned about the missing classified documents that pertained to his work. He documented the grave event and complained about it. I saw several scripts of the same letter, some written as a draft in haste, documenting quickly what happened, and later other more detailed neater versions. I could immediately see the anger, shock and revulsion he felt at what people in his office had done during his absence.

How high and elevated, how esteemed and sincere, to react spontaneously and so intensely about what is right and wrong and to say it and document it. That's what honest people do. They react with their gut and they say what is wrong. Dad wrote immediately to his director and copied the correspondence to several other important officials, as high as the minister of telecommunications and transportation.

In those letters, Dad stated what happened and who might have done it — based on the word of an eyewitness. Why might these people do such a horrible thing? There were important projects under Dad's supervision. They pertained to wireless and wired communication for a secret radar defense system, a secret wireless switchboard for the presidential palace and its relevant codes, telecommunication security and confidential employee files. As a professional and as a sincere citizen, Dad was duly concerned about the security of these materials, and he exhibited the

السيد المدير العام

عند رجوعي من سفري خارج العراق ومباشرتي من الدائرة: صباح ليوم ١٥ / ١٠ / ١٩٦٨ لاحظت ان المسفنة التي استثنى علاء عادل: قد دفعت مع طائفة المحزات التالفة لا والتي تحتوي على الد ضبارات السريه ومحابرات متفرقة ومحتويات تخصه علما بان طائفة هذه المحزات كانت مقفوده سلا من تزويج هامي وعندما استفسرت من المرات المسؤول مهدي اعلمني بان الطابه الذلكورة قد دفعت من قبل السيد عبدالحميد سعيد وانه قد كسر جميع المحزات و لعرفت لقسم من محتويا لا ولما كان هذا العمل يعتبر اعتداء على حرمة الدائرة وللكها وان صونف خارج المرات وانه لعرفت شان لدليق شخص المقرون من الله يحمل سري د هامه مهه من خارج المرات وان كسر المحزات قد ذكرت رحمي لعتبر هذه لقصد السرقه كما انه ليس له اي حق بم منزل المرته كهذا الشكل واللعرفت كهذا الاسلوب الثاني لذا ارجو التفضل با حالة الموضوع الى لجنة التحلق لاجراء التحقيق بذلك وا خذ افاده المزام مهدي و المحنف منزر الكوجه والذي كان قابعا باعمالي طلية صدة غيابي .

[signature]

صوره منه الى :
١٥ / ١٠ / ١٩٦٨
رئيس المنتسبين

رئيس هيئه الرقابيه المسكريه من معطيه الدين والدين وللكانف

با لنظر لسرقه بعض الدوائر السريه والملفات العائد لسرالة العفر الحميزيني السريه وغيرها من المحابرات التي نظلق بلادمه المواصلات السلكيه واللا سلكيه خا رجو اتخاذ ما لزم من مهزتكم لقدر ما تقتضيا الامر يكم .

Truths that Dad wrote so innocently and so persistently about the event during which his office was broken into and confidential documents were taken. The documents that were stolen pertained to communication systems for the presidential palace and intelligence relating to wireless and wired communications. (This story is related in my previous book, *The First Evidence*.) I love Dad's signature.

125

highest standards of professionalism and ethics. He quickly, openly, and transparently reported the incident to his superiors and requested an immediate inquiry into this matter. As I read those documents for the first time more than forty years after they were written, I realized that Dad had done exactly what I would have expected him to do.

I know that feeling. I have been there too. I know the anger one feels when one sees wrong. The urgency to tell your superiors or those concerned, the urgency to warn about what might happen, and the disgust you feel that people you know or with whom you work or interact have done these horrible things. I am stunned, just like Dad was forty-four years ago, that people are dishonest in their work, plotting and scheming, caring nothing for the public interest. I did exactly the same thing as my father when I encountered corrupt actions, before even having seen those documents. I too saw shocking things from some individuals, and I too wrote to those concerned, and I too emphasized how harmful such behavior is to the public interest.

I had only known Dad when I was a child. When I became a young adult, I was living far away, and Dad was ill. Then he had his major stroke and was bedridden; then he passed away. So it was that I did not really interact with him when I was an adult. I did not get to talk deeply with him regarding life matters, professional matters or other important things. So it delights me today to read the various memos and documents that he had prepared decades ago about many different serious subjects, from his arrest ordeal to trying to regain his position to some events at his work, in addition to some matters related to our family and our house. As I read through those documents, I learned about my dad and, to my utmost delight, I discovered that I am just like him. I am meticulous, and I stand up against wrong.

I do remember well that Dad was organized and meticulous about his documents. His study at home was full of shelves, file cabinets, books and documents. I used to go there and sit with him as he worked, but I did not touch any of those files. Only now do I have some of these documents in my possession and look at them carefully. And when I go through them, I see how much I am like my dad: detail oriented, and unafraid to speak up or document in writing what I think. I, too, am persistent about matters that are important and significant — and like Dad, I do not give up.

It would have been so good to know about him while he was alive and tell him about my life and seek his guidance. I never knew that I am like Dad in dealing with work and life until I faced professional dilemmas later in my life and until I read those documents. I never talked to him about what he faced at work. I was a child when he had his ordeal in the 1970s and when he was confronting these other work challenges such as having his desk broken into. When I was nineteen and he was ill, I spent a few months with him and Mom in London but we were mostly concerned with his illness and we did not delve into these work related issues in detail.

I see his righteousness first hand, pure and daring. I see his bold and accurate representation of facts and his assessment of the wrong that he saw. How powerful are his words as I read them now, so many

A lovely photograph of Dad in his twenties.

years later. Simple truths written, documented, meant for me to find decades later, to study and investigate. So many things from our house got lost or stolen or were dispersed with different relatives. The house itself was demolished, as I described earlier. My mom had prepared so many beautiful things for us kids, for when we grew up and got married. She had bought for us precious fabrics, jewelry, and things for our would-be babies. Most of these things did not survive; none of them reached me, at least. But the precious documents were salvaged so that I could see them and tell the world about them.

Carved into these documents that were so important and dear to my dad are his idealism, his honesty, his sincerity, and his meticulousness and authenticity in stating the facts and relating what happened and why he is reporting it. His high ethics and integrity, pure and bold, stand out very clearly on the old, cracking paper.

I am grateful more than ever to Mom and Dad for teaching me rock-solid pure values. That I find out today how much like dad I am is the most important thing that I know about myself today. I am so privileged to be that way, and I would not trade the values I learned for anything or any amount of dollars. Let me tell you why. It is very simple. Righteousness to me is equivalent to the coherence of my thinking, to the clarity of my mind and to the spontaneity of friendships and relationships. It is the normal status of my soul and my body. I do not know how to be other than that way. It is so pleasurable that I cannot find words to explain what I mean.

And I feel sorrow and pity for all those deceitful people, whether now during my lifetime or those who harmed my dad years ago, because they cannot even be themselves. They must always think about how to manage their lies and put them together into any shape they fit. They are constantly worried about how to keep from spelling out their lies by accident, how to beautify them, and how to act so that they will not be discovered. They must always patch and paste what they do in order to hide their wrong. I feel pity for such low souls who are willing to lose their spontaneity, pleasure, clarity and coherence and must live in the underworld of deception and kiss up to others just for some petty *or* hefty benefit.

I am delighted and honored to find out, at the height of my career, that I am a replica of my dad not only in his ethics but also his meticulousness. I am meticulous too. I am thorough and careful about the work that I do, whatever it is, and I stand high as he did by values. Today, everyone who knows me would agree that I do not tolerate wrong, not even for one second. I do not accept it. I oppose it. I stop it as much as I can. I say it out loud. I am sorry if some people call that undiplomatic. I just call it being assertive, caring about what you believe in and caring about public interest. I never hide any wrong that I know about under the rug. Yes indeed, it harms me personally, and I reap no material benefits from being righteous. But it is the right thing to do, and this is how I am and I am very happy about it. Although I do not gain anything this way, I get tremendous pleasure by doing what is right: a clear conscience and peace of mind, knowing that whatever money I make, I have earned it. And maybe, too, I am silently, quietly and very humbly an inspiration of courage and adherence to ethics to others.

Everyone who knows me today would also agree that I am meticulous, to the point of being obsessive about it, and I do not like sloppy work. Some friends do call me, jokingly, obsessive. Or maybe they do mean it!

I also discovered from those documents — and also, regrettably, from my own experience in life — that these battles against evil exist in all times, across generations and in many countries. Corruption and opportunism existed before in Iraq, and my dad opposed it, and he suffered because of that. And today the same plagues are prevalent in Iraq and many people are harmed by them. Indeed, opportunists and people with no morals and no ethics are all over the world, not just in Iraq. They justify doing wrong and could not care less. These people are driven by their raw desires. They do not exercise their logic and reason — maybe because they do not have any. I think people who have ethics and morals have them because of the pure and elevated way they were brought up *and* because of the self-discipline and control that they have over their behavior. High discipline comes from things like intense exercise, or intense prayer or mediations, or fasting. These things indeed do give us self-control and put a check on raw human behavior. How brave and kind dad was in his mid-career (as well as later, at the pinnacle of his career) to be confronted by mafias and people with personal agendas and to have the courage to expose it!

Although we cannot change people's personal conduct, especially when they are old, we can see how other countries deal with such corruption problems and even how they were dealt with in Iraq before, say, decades ago. Based on what I learned from my experience in the United States, the way to deal with corruption and dishonesty is by having protocols and procedures in all sectors of work. Further, we can establish checks and audits throughout the work environment to detect and deter such violations. In addition, of course, we can teach people both at home and in work settings about ethics, accountability and respecting public interest.

* * *

After his ordeal in late 1973 and onward after his release from prison, Dad struggled to obtain his rights and to exonerate his name from the Ba'ath accusations. He wrote some pleas to various officials about his ordeal and his innocence. He tried to resume his employment. He affirmed over and over his innocence. Although he was punished unjustly by the regime, actually he received an official clearance or exoneration document several months after he was released from prison. He was given that because he had never violated any laws as documented through the normal legal system and police records of those times. Some aspects of the government ran normally in spite of the Ba'ath regime, and not everything was corrupted immediately at the same time.

In spite of these efforts, Dad was unable to get his high ranking position back. He spent several years mostly working as freelancer, teaching at institutes of higher education. During those years his health was deteriorating.

But there is more in those documents of Ba'ath corruption and evil. The Egyptian maid, Jasmine, who used to work in our house, was corresponding with her husband back in Egypt through the Ba'ath government. Her name was different from what we knew, "Jasmine." That was her fake name or "mission" name! Her real name was Samara. I also found a letter that her husband in Egypt had sent to her. It is noticeable on the letter that the first two or three lines are written in a different tone as well as a different handwriting. It seems that the letter was manipulated.

* * *

It saddens me again as I read those details and as I am writing about them. I wish there was something I could have done for Dad and Mom during those turbulent times of our life. Actually these subjects, and others in the documents I have, are important to me, and I intend to spend the rest of my life investigating them and getting to the bottom of what really happened. Some of the people involved are still alive. Even the maid and her husband might still be alive. But that will be the subject of later work.

But I discovered something else. It is not just about Dad, but about Iraq. It is about humanity. It makes me further proud of my dad and of following in his footsteps. He was a stellar professional. He was a star. He had amazing professional achievements and far-reaching successes. Dad led many professional teams during the 1950s and the 1960s. He managed huge programs and represented Iraq in many professional meetings and conferences. Among the documents I have are one nomination decree after another selecting Dad to take charge of these different programs or to represent Iraq in many scientific and professional workshops and conferences all over the world, including meetings of Arab and international organizations. He was a key figure in the telecommunication field, not just in Iraq but also in the region. I learned that he established the network and communication system for some countries in the region and ran many projects in that regard. He shared his knowledge and talents with the region. Not only did he serve Iraq, but also he helped several other countries develop. How inspiring and amazing that is.

Iraqi professionals like my dad helped the region in many scientific and educational endeavors. I also remember that my aunt was sent on assignment to Kuwait to be a teacher or a school head because they did not have teachers! Many of our family friends and our relatives who were doctors and engineers and teachers were sent on assignments to various Arab countries to teach and to heal and to build. This is what Iraqis did not too long ago. While Iraq had been deteriorating over the past three decades, Iraqi expatriates were building other countries. They were teaching all over the globe and reaching high positions in their fields of expertise. As long as Iraq does not appreciate its expatriate experts and talented people abroad, it will not recover.

It is ironic that nearly half a century later, the countries built by Iraqi talents like my dad now provide aid or aid platforms to Iraq to rebuild various aspects of its economic and technical enterprises. And today many of these countries are still run by Iraqi expatriates who live all over the world and in nearby countries.

When talented experts leave their native land it is called brain drain. It is bad for countries and it must be reversed. Iraq needs these experts to come back. Iraq needs them to work, teach, heal, and be key figures in making the present and the future. This has not happened yet. In addition, Iraq needs experts and talented people *who are also sincere* and who work with the goal of helping Iraq and improving the lives of its people. Here, again, I pay tribute to my parents and to their generation for doing amazing things not just for us, their children, but for other countries and societies. I thank them for raising us properly, for instilling values in us, for giving us strong roots, for providing a good life as much as circumstances allowed and many other things. I am not sure that my generation has been able to give any of those values or even the lifestyle to their children.

I do not see elements of a solid foundation and high values in today's young generation. I want my words to preserve whatever little is left of these older sentiments. I do not mean to be pessimistic and look only to the past as some will accuse me. Actually the past is not only important but very inspirational to me. I do not look down on the past of anything. I use it as a guide. I do think that we should look forward and move on. But I feel very strongly that one must know and understand the past, learn its good lessons, and use them as a foundation for the future. And I do not even mind indulging a little in admiring the good things of the past. I always ask my colleagues and friends, if our parents were able to achieve amazing things with far fewer resources and far less advanced technology fifty and sixty years ago, why can't we do better or even the same when we have access to high technology and much more resources (not to mention to all the foreign help coming to us)? This is what I ask as I look at various proposals to help lift Iraq's education or healthcare or agriculture. Why is it that we were able to do all those things really well before and now we can't? These questions are ones we must ask ourselves every day.

My parents' generation did not have magic. They had three important elements that made them successful: sincerity, good planning, and reasonable resources. I think today in Iraq, we have little sincerity and lots of poor planning. Yet we have plenty of resources. The oil revenues and the foreign aid are ample.

But we do have mismanagement and poor planning — I should say, *no* planning in some cases. Iraq needs a major overhaul in its planning and execution of all projects, and Iraqis need wise planning with sincerity and progress in mind.

I share here just one minuscule example. I attended an event at the Alrasheed Hotel in early 2012. Because many VIPs and dignitaries attended this event, there was supposedly high security. So they asked everyone to empty their pockets or purses of pens, flash drives, lighters and items like that. The organizers must have not thought about the consequences. They just told everyone (that's hundreds of people) to put their items on a table, and the items just piled up and up until they mad a little hill of pens, lighters, and so on. But no one had thought of how people were going to get their items back when they left the event. They had not even thought of bringing some Ziploc bags and giving one to each person with a number attached on the bag. At least this way people could collect their items in a reasonable manner. All it would have taken was a little bit of thinking in advance about all the steps. (It is called planning!) At the end of the event, all the items were mixed up and people had to search for their pens and lighter as things fell off the table.

Something as simple as organizing a conference and running the logistics of it has become difficult to do these days. I keep telling my Iraqi friends how in the U.S. events always run properly and on time and smoothly. Every detail is planned out. Everyone respects his or her part of the work whether it is collecting trash, giving out handouts or doing a security check. Events always run well and do their intended purpose.

I am not the only one missing the goodness of the older times of our parents and our grandparents. Many people I met in Iraq have the same sentiments. I met several prominent wonderful people who knew my parents in various capacities. I have already mentioned meeting a friend of my brothers who spoke of his love for our family home, and another family friend who has put me in touch with his daughter in the U.S. Another prominent man I met was formerly a student of my dad's in university. I am so honored and happy to have met all those esteemed people. I am sure there are hundreds of others whom I did not see because of the difficulty of moving around freely in Baghdad.

I also met a family friend from some thirty-five years ago. Actually she was a friend of my sister but I knew her too. She was then and still is now a good, spirited, active, inspiring woman to be with. It was amazing to see her after all those years. She was as energetic and lively as ever, doing great things with orphans and needy people. It is such a delight to see wonderful, sincere people working hard to make things better for others.

* * *

A Sea of Graves

I had never been to a cemetery in Iraq before. Visiting the cemeteries is a part of traditions in Iraq, as it is elsewhere, but I am not well versed in this tradition because I did not go to cemeteries as a child. Normally people go visit their loved ones in cemeteries, especially during the *Eid* occasions (i.e., the holidays) and at other times too, particularly to commemorate the date of someone's passing away. People visit and pray for their loved ones who passed away and take greenery and flowers. But cemeteries are not the same in Iraq as they are in the United States. They are more deserted and not easily accessible. You have to sort of arrange to go visit the graves. You cannot just go there at your convenience. Sometimes the cemeteries are locked and you have to find the attendant.

Wadi al Salam cemetery, where my parents were laid to rest, is in the Holy City of Najaf (about 100 miles south of Baghdad).[2] It is truly a one-of-a-kind place. It is unique because of its location, size, and history. It is located near the Imam Ali Shrine[3]—which makes the city of Najaf the Holy City of Najaf. The cemetery is huge by all measures. It looks like a sea of graves. As far as one looks and in all directions, one sees grave upon grave. This enormous cemetery is more than fourteen hundred years old. Shia Muslims from all over the world seek to be buried there because it is near the Shrine of Imam Ali. People write in their wills to be buried there. They believe this is a blessed land and that if you are laid to rest there you will be saved. It is kind of like a safe haven where you do not suffer during purgatory.

Although an eerie city of the dead and the weeping, the cemetery is actually remarkable. It makes you think about death and dying. It makes you realize how small this life is. Any of us could just perish any moment. We do not even know when. Hundreds of thousands of graves, side by side and even on top of each other; lots of names and signs and notices about where people rest. The place is also unusual because it is very crowded and disorganized. It is not well kept. No one takes care of cleaning it and there is no grass, no trees, no plants of any sort. During my one or two visits there, I immediately started asking why they don't make a picture map of the place with some main landmarks so that it will be easier for people to navigate their way.

The staff who work there at the graveyard have their work cut out for them, because nearly all Shia Muslims seek the place as I mentioned above. The staff—actually it is more like a family business—do many duties. They are the ones who transport the dead and comfort people during and after the burial. They prepare the burial site. The burial has a special set of rituals. Usually the male family members and relatives of the deceased go through it with the aid of those workers or volunteers. But women go later, after weeks and months, and normally visit their loved ones regularly and during many religious holidays. They do not participate directly in the burial proceedings.

Special traditions and customs govern the visits to the graves, just as they govern each stage of our lives from when we are born until we die and even after die. I learned the traditions of visiting the cemeteries and practiced them for the first time. First, most people go to the Holy City of Najaf early in the day to avoid traffic and to avoid the heat in the summer, and also of course to avoid being there in the late hours. At the cemetery, people sit at the gravesite. They light candles and incense. They rinse the tomb or the wall of the grave with rosewater. They sit and weep or read the Holy Quran and recite prayers. Or they just sit there reflecting. I did these things too. At the gravesites, some caretaker men stand nearby. They join you to read the Quran and read some prayers. Usually they stay there, at the cemetery. They are not really employees; they assist people in opening up the gates and reaching the graves, and they read Quran and some prayers. Usually they get some charity money or food that the family members have brought with them. It is also normal for people to visit the graves on Fridays (which is the weekend).

I stood amidst thousands of graves. It was wonderful but eerie. There are graves all around you wherever you look. It is like drowning in a sea of graves and names. Although there are many visitors, things are very quiet. It seems everyone is busy reciting and reflecting. Everyone is hidden near the grave of his or her loved one.

When I arrived at the cemetery for the first time, I could not visit the graves of Mom and Dad because I did not know exactly where to go in the huge cemetery. I had to contact the caretaker and research with him where the burial site of my parents was. None of my siblings had been there before, so I could not ask them. (My siblings are abroad, too; some of them have visited Iraq for short periods of time.) And although my uncle and my aunts, who live in Iraq, had been there before and were there during the burial, that was a long time ago — maybe soon after the passing of my parents. In recent years no one had been there. They too have gotten old and it is not that easy for them to travel to Najaf.

I could not find the burial site right away, but I knew that I was near my parents, even though they rest in their graves as they have for more than twenty years. I was close — but not close enough. I was anxious to reach them.

We drove through the main alleys of the cemetery, and then we had to stop the car and continue on foot because the alleys became smaller and could not fit a car. We walked amidst graves. We reached the place, and we had to go down some steps. This is how the burial sites are designed. All I shall say is that it very hard to see your parents' graves, to see their names on the tombs. It was almost surreal. I would like to be able to stay there for hours and even days, contemplating life and remembering them. However, it is hard to arrange for such a visit. The whole cemetery setting is not designed for long visits, and the weather also does not permit staying long.

Mom and Dad were true soul mates. When Mom passed away, Dad followed rather soon. As much as it was hard and sad for me and my siblings to lose both parents in a short time period, it was sweet and touching to see that my Dad loved my Mom so much that his life was hard without her. True lovers are like that. They want to be with each other.

I prayed and I read parts of the Quran and sat there for a while. But I felt close and comfortable. Visiting the grave was an important milestone for me and a big accomplishment because it was hard to go there and hard to find, and it was something that I wanted to do and sought for many months after I came to Iraq. I tried hard to find my way there, and, with the help of my husband and his family, I was able to go there. I am grateful to them. I feel rested, having found what I long sought.

NOTES

1. This happens in Iraq, unfortunately. Whenever people see an empty home or an empty lot, they use it, and sometimes it is hard to get them to leave. Initially, many years ago, there was a guard at the house; however, when the security situation became lax, even the guard was afriad for his life. So it became more or less deserted.

2. Although my parents passed away in the United Kingdom, they had advised previously that they be laid to rest in the Holy City of Najaf, and such arrangements were made at the time of their passing.

3. Imam Ali is the first of the twelve Shia Imams.

CHAPTER IV

For Better or for Worse: Iraqis and Americans

Iron and Steel

I am glad that I came to Iraq. I came with the intention to help Iraq recover and move forward, to fix things and make them better. I had to do this. I had to give it a try. I do believe that not many things are impossible and that we can achieve many good things if there are good people willing to work and to try. Was it worth it, what I did to come back after so many years? Yes, absolutely. Was it hard? Yes, absolutely. I had to use all my patience, all my tolerance, all the zeal and energy that I had. I had to become iron and steel in order to survive here. Do I regret coming here? No, not at all. Would I do it again? Yes.

I am very grateful to have this added experience in my life, and I am grateful to have had the opportunity to contribute something that will bring positive change and progress to Iraq. Now that I have done this — given my skills and knowledge, contributed to make things work here, done my best to help Iraq improve education for young people, done my best to guide and to inspire the people I saw — I feel that I am done for now. I did what I can, and I hope it will bring good results one day.

And while I was at it, I made a new life in Iraq. I made some amazing new friends, both Iraqis and Americans. They have added new happiness and new insight in my life. They have touched my heart. It is sweet to have met new Iraqis with whom I totally got along and who appreciated my friendship and experience. And it is also sweet and delightful to have met some Americans in Iraq and befriended them. I felt very close to them because they talk like me, they are straightforward, they are not that complex to deal with, they understand when I say I miss certain things about the U.S., and some of them helped me get a few American things.

And I would like to announce, firsthand to the whole world, that I adjusted okay after being away for thirty years. I like to say that it was hard but not impossible. Both my husband and I adjusted all right. And no, we did not have "reverse cultural shock"—whatever that is—which many Iraqis and Arabs seem to speak of and to suffer from after spending only three or four years abroad!

Adjusting to the living conditions in Iraq is only a small part of the story. Indeed, it is the easy part of being in the new Iraq. I think you do have to be tough to survive here in addition to having a sense of humor. I wrote many parts of this book in the cold. One night in January there was a cold front in Iraq. The temperature was around zero Celsius (about 32°F) and there was no electricity and no water. It was hard, but I tolerated it. This situation continued some sixteen hours and the apartment became freezing cold. I lit some candles to try to get some heat going. It was hard to find other means of heat such as kerosene operated heaters because the kerosene was hard to transport into the IZ. That was indeed hard. In my new lifestyle, I am now used to the electric power problem, checkpoints, having to show my ID everywhere I go, and so on. All these things are now part of my life.

Adjusting to the living conditions was hard but doable, but it was *easy* compared to opposing ills like deceit, favoritism, and the pursuit of personal agendas over the good of society or the good of a cause. To survive these circumstances, you have be made of iron and steel. You have to the nerve and guts to do what is right, to say it loud and clear and do whatever it takes. And I did all that. I do have guts. It was hard. It took a toll on my health and well being. But this is the new Iraq, with its virtues and vices. You must have tremendous stamina in order to keep going.

I have learned about the limits of my endurance. I have exercised my resilience and sharpened my patience. I endured days with no running water. I learned to collect water in containers and save it for such days. I endured the no-electric-power experience and learned to love the little current of air from the battery-operated table-top fan that we bought. That fan is so cool. It ran for about two hours on battery. But when it too stopped, I endured the blistering 120°F or so degree heat. I learned to wash my vegetables and fruits thoroughly with soap and a brush, or I peel or cook them.

All in all, my two years of hard work and hopeful enthusiasm were highly stressful and somewhat disappointing. I had never had so much stress in my life. Nearly daily I was intensely stressed by someone's rudeness, incompetence, negligence or apathy. Throughout the past two or so years, I heard many discouraging remarks from well meaning and not so well meaning people: you can't survive there, you can't achieve anything, you are wasting your time, you don't know anything about Iraq, and so on. These comments are not nice and I did not appreciate them.

The new Iraq broke my heart and shocked me many times. The new Iraq made me cry and made me ill. I was sad to see people reminiscing about the old days and how things were better as far as healthcare and education and some services. I was shocked by the negligence, apathy and waste. I was shocked by how careless people are about their health. I was upset about the poverty and the scene of poor children in the streets and the extreme wealth (*new* wealth, I might add) of the politicians on the other hand.

It is sad to see that some people brush off these disparities and do not wish to talk about them. It shocked me to see that important issues like these are let go, either because these are touchy subjects and political groups do not want to upset each other, or because of some benefit someone might get in position, money or other rewards if he keeps his mouth shut. I stressed over this issue and it worried me a lot. It kept me awake at night, thinking about evil acts that people do so they may reap benefits for themselves while harming Iraq.

Although the work I am involved in is not itself hard compared to what I used to work on when I did scientific research, the overall environment brought me severe levels of stress and agony. I am used to tough situations. I worked hard before when I was in the U.S., I handled many different tasks, worked long hours and was very happy and enthusiastic. I used to handle radioactive materials, toxic chemicals and contaminated blood, but I was relaxed and calm. I am sure I was stressed out here and there once in a while. But I do not ever remember being chronically and intensely stressed and dealing with so much negligence and carelessness.

I discovered the hard way how difficult it is to stand alone to do what is right, and how hard it is to do what is right amidst self-serving and careless individuals. I also saw, face to face, the ugliness of favoritism, nepotism, negligence and apathy. I dealt harshly with these issues. I stood against them. I tried to educate those around me about work ethics. I hope that, one day, the seeds of ethics and excellence I planted will grow into beautiful trees and flowers of sincerity and honesty.

But it is sad that there are people who reached the point of despair, believing that things will not change for the better. Particularly I saw this in some people who are sincere and hard working but are being lost amidst the chaos of favoritism and corruption. A few I saw have given up. Some are from within Iraq and others have come from abroad like I did. But they have given up, and some have quit. Some of them asked for my help. I told them to be patient and to keep steadfast. But everyone has a finite level of tolerance. I do not blame them for quitting. It is hard being in Iraq. Good, sincere people are not welcome sometimes. On the contrary, they are fought and are not appreciated. The current circumstances almost kill enthusiasm. I say "almost" because I am not pessimistic.

It is a big debate in Iraq: Whenever you mention people coming from abroad, all kinds of conclusions pop up. People say that those who came from abroad (like me) cannot withstand the high temperatures and the poor living conditions, or that they will never come, or that they come and immediately go back. I definitely can say that this is the wrong argument. It is not the living conditions that we who came from abroad cannot withstand. It is not the lack of water or the lack of electricity; I myself took that quite well. I adapted to and accepted the conditions as they are. But it is the corruption, the favoritism, the nepotism, the lack of transparency and the prevailing ignorance that those who come from abroad cannot stand and cannot live with.

One side issue about expatriate Iraqis is something I feel especially sad about. Some expatriates have gotten enmeshed in marital problems or even have gotten divorced after coming to Iraq. Many expatriates came back to Iraq alone, leaving their families back where they are living (e.g., Europe, North America, or Iran). Well, soon some of these people got remarried in Iraq and they got divorced from their spouse at home. It is sad to hear about that. And it is one more challenge that expatriates have to deal with.

But back to the experience of expatriates: I myself felt the antagonism against expatriate Iraqis that I alluded to. I was upset and disappointed many times but never to the point of losing hope. I do not lose hope. I am optimistic because of my faith and my personality. I do not give up easily. It is just my nature. I do not want to exaggerate and say I never give up, but it does not happen often. And the very same Iraq which broke my heart gave me reasons to hope. The same Iraq gave me reasons to stay here and to keep going and not give up.

There are sincere people in Iraq who do care and do the right thing. There are indeed enough good people out there who will not yield to external pressures or even to their own personal desires. There is a proverb from Imam Ali that may be paraphrased as *Right will not prevail unless there are people who seek to achieve it.* Definitely and positively, in spite of all the wrong things I saw, there were shining pockets of goodness, of sincerity, of innocence. There were and are smart sincere people who are working hard and who are giving their heart and soul to make things better. For example, in their families, Iraqis maintain their strong ties. They prepare festive meals in spite of lack of facilities and poor conditions. I saw these things every day. I also saw many charity projects and much good will. I saw little children who were *not* begging but working small jobs such as cleaning windshields of cars in the streets. Actually, it broke my heart to see that because they were just kids and they were so small sometimes they could not even reach the car; but it is a good value to work and earn your money. I know these kids will be resilient when they grow up.

And there are more good stories too. One of the nicest compliments I got in Iraq was from a colleague who came a few times to our office — always at the same time, first thing in the morning — to assist with some project. He was a professor, an older gentleman, and I did not know him from before. He had studied in the United States decades ago, maybe before I was born. In the few times that he saw me, he told me, "I could not help noticing that you are always working first thing in the morning and you do not waste any time. Most other people in this office" — and, he said, elsewhere in Iraq, based on his long standing experience — "just hang out, chat, and eat, and they work only when they are told to work." This was the sweetest compliment that I got. I told him that this is what I learned from being in the United States, that I care about my work and take it seriously and this is how I always work. I worked hard when I first started my career. I did not make a lot of money necessarily — certainly not during my first steps of work — and this is how it was. But I was always happy and excited about my work and I was happy to learn many things. The compliment from this colleague was really sweet and made me happy.

Further, I always feel happy when I see kids playing and having fun, in spite of the poor conditions around them, and in spite of the very little they have. That's my style too. Make the best out of any situation no matter how hard it is. There are many people who have good values and great will, and they just need support and they will do great things. When I think of these people and these kids and how their lives will change if I and people like me do nothing, then I have more resolve. When good, sincere people stop their efforts and give up, evil flourishes. When good, sincere people work hard and persevere, evil diminishes and withers away.

I indeed have hope. I have a lot of hope. I never gave up hope, not for one second. Yes, I got tired and frustrated many times. I was often disappointed by the people around me and their behavior. Sure, several people were rude and unappreciative and maybe had other motives too. But I think you find such disappointments everywhere and every time. As I mentioned earlier, although I was angry and frustrated many times, I always try to make sweetness and beauty around me in order to relax and feel better. I try to enjoy the beauty of my moment and the beauty of what is around me. I look out the window and appreciate the sky or the sun, I light candles, I use incense, I bring flowers and put them where I can see them. All of these things made me relaxed amidst very harsh conditions.

* * *

My being here did not fix all problems in Iraq. I contributed something small. I did what I could to make things better. I inspired a few people, I taught others, I pushed people to think for the good of Iraq and to do things well, I scrubbed the "rust" from some people's ideas and actions. And I am sure that at least in some people, I ignited their passion for doing their work with excellence, doing what is right, standing with the righteous truthful side of many issues. And that alone is enough and satisfactory to me and is worth a million dollars. It gives me great pleasure that I showed some people how to do their work well and correctly and pointed out wrong loudly and clearly when I saw it . I was brought up — in the old Iraq — with these moral values which I preserved and further developed in the United States, where I learned essential work values and professional ethics.

* * *

Between Cultures and Generations

Iraq and the United States are blended in me. I love them both. I am a reflection of both. I understand both countries. I want those two great countries to get along in their new "arranged marriage."

When I came to the United States as a teenager in the early 1980s, hardly anyone knew where my home country was. At that time, Iraq was some unknown region to most of the Americans I knew. There was not much mention of Iraq even in the news in spite of the onslaught, at that time, of the first Gulf War, the Iran–Iraq war throughout the 1980s. I never envisioned at that time that, some three decades later, Iraq and the United States would be having such a profound impact on each other, with results likely to last a lifetime or more. I never envisioned that our fates would be so intertwined for decades yet to come as if both of our countries conceded to an arranged marriage. I am at the center of this marriage, and it is people like me who can make this arranged marriage work. I love Iraq and I love the United States and would love to bounce back and forth between these two great places that made me who I am. I want to make things better for people in Iraq and in the United States.

I have lived in the United States since the age of sixteen, and I managed my American life without parental guidance as my parents could not be in the U.S. due to the political problems in Iraq since then. I came here with my sister, who was seventeen, and we both stayed with our brother, who was in his mid-twenties and was living in the States before we came. Our experience is rather unusual and contrasts with that of most of the Iraqi American community who have come to the United States either as adults in their twenties and thirties (in which case they were shaped mostly by their Iraqi heritage) or as babies (in which case they do not know much about Iraq).

I am proud to have lived in the United States and learned and enjoyed great things that the country gave me and never neglected my values and religion. I am grateful to have lived in the U.S. and very proud to say that I never touched drugs or alcohol as many immigrant kids and foreign students often do when they first come to America. I did not have a boyfriend. I did not go to parties. I did not skip one day of my Muslim prayers. I did not skip any Ramadan fasting; on the contrary, I had great Ramadan experiences in the United States, many times along with American friends. I am grateful to have lived in such a country that allowed people to be they way they are and to practice their religion and assimilate without demanding that anyone change their name, their hair color or the way they dress. And this is the first thing I would like Iraqis to know about the United States: Americans are very accommodating people, and with them you can be yourself the way you are and they are happy to accept you.

* * *

Notwithstanding my strong Iraqi roots and my serious adherence to the primary values that I learned from Iraq, I am very American. I, too, like Americans, accept people as they are and respect any differences they may have with me or with my lifestyle. I do all the daily American things: I have to get coffee in the morning, I hang out at the mall, I recycle paper and plastic water bottles, I go to the gym, I love long weekends, and I very much love the holiday season. I love Thanksgiving and the exciting feelings we have on the Wednesday before Thanksgiving in anticipation of the holiday, and I love the holiday rush hour traffic. I love how the snow flurries hit your face in winter, and I love to walk in the slushy roads where the snow is beginning to melt. I love the dramatic, windy weather in Florida and how the sky and the water turn into the same shade of grey when the intense clouds gather quickly and the rain starts. And I especially like the fall season in the northeastern parts of the United States with the magnificently colored tree leaves falling on the ground, hitting it with a gentle sound and layering it like a beautiful rug with gorgeous colors.

* * *

At the same time, the Iraq I came from is not equal to all the stereotypes that we — Americans — have about the Middle East. And it is definitely not equal to what people saw of Iraq immediately after the war and continue to see: the looting, the beheading and the long anticipated and talked about "civil war" between Shias and Sunnis. As I have already said, we in Iraq have not been "killing each other for generations," as it is always depicted in the news. And if civil war were something we had been fearing for centuries as the "experts" and the media like to say, then we would have heard about it from our grandfathers and grandmothers and elders, and the supposed horrors would have aroused visceral fear and rage in us every time we heard the names Shia and Sunni. But we never had such fear of each other, and we do not commonly use the term "civil war." The only visceral fear we all had in Iraq was a fear of the Ba'ath government and what they might do next.

It is neither logical nor fair to reduce all of Iraq's history, civilization and contribution to humanity to the weeks of looting and chaos that took place in April 2003 under awkward, suspicious circumstances that were never investigated. It is neither accurate nor fair to characterize Iraq by the actions of the hooligans we all saw on television a few days after the war, when in fact the overwhelming majority of people were at home and in their neighborhoods maintaining peace and calm. It is as illogical and unfair to categorize all Iraqis by looting, chaos and "civil war" as it is to categorize all Americans by what happened in the Abu Ghraib prison fiasco. Unfortunately, to both Iraqis and Americans, first impressions do matter most.

Americans and Iraqis have always formulated their views about each other based on very generalized regional stereotypes. Iraqis — and Arabs in general — tend to think of all westerners as one group in spite of the vast differences between the various countries, and in spite of the fact that Europeans and Americans think that they are different from each other, and in spite of the fact that within Europe and within the United States there are significant regional differences. For example, in the United States there are significant differences between the lifestyle of the Midwest region and the lifestyle of the western states or the South. Similarly, Americans tend to think of "the Middle East" or "the Muslim world" as one big group of people in spite of the enormous differences in history, culture, languages and current politics of various countries in the region.

* * *

I come back in my thoughts to my life experience in the United States and how it prepared me to serve Iraq. I have yet another 30 years away from another place that I love. It has been nearly thirty years since I first came to the United States, to Ohio. I was there in the early and mid–1980s. It is there that I learned many things in life. It is there that I actually experimented with cooking. It is there that I learned about baked potatoes and Thanksgiving. It is there that I first attended college, there that I learned driving and set foot in a university for the first time. I ache now to go visit all the places that I used to go in Ohio. The roads, the freeways, the restaurants and so many other things. I like to go there to visit and to look at the same places three decades later. I am very much missing a drive on the freeways between the small towns in Ohio where I have so many wonderful memories from my teens. And of course I miss Los Angeles. I miss the restaurants, I miss my friends, I miss the freeways, the traffic — I love L.A. traffic! I miss American food and American coffee. I miss going to the gym. I am so lucky to love both Iraq and the U.S. and to find pleasure in both and to miss them both when I am away.

One thing that keeps frustrating me is that there are few people in my shoes. Not many people have been through the same circumstances that I have experienced. It makes it hard for most people around me to understand my perspective, and it makes me feel like no one hears what I am saying. Many times when I say things, they are very far ahead from what people are thinking. It is like speaking on another wavelength. I try my best, however, to be in other people's shoes. I listen very attentively and carefully to anyone who talks to me. I am happy to say that I am a good listener and in that regard I am more like Americans — they listen !— than Iraqis. But I do not feel that people see my viewpoints and understand where I come from.

Many of the Iraqis and Iraqi Americans I know, either in the U.S. or in Iraq, are older than me or younger than me. Hardly any of my peers have led a life similar to mine and have done what I have. Therefore, in many instances I am ahead of people, and in others I am very far away from what they are doing. When I talk to older Iraqis, they talk to me about the fifties and the sixties and about their retirement and pension and things like that. They expect me to understand their viewpoint, and I try my best to do so, but I do not relate directly to such issues because I am not their age. When I talk to young people they do not have the original perspective about how things were in Iraq. I do not blame them. They lived in Iraq and all they saw was war and destruction and lack of freedoms and poverty and so on. Their interests are different. And the younger Iraqis or foreign born Iraqis who are abroad are too detached from Iraq; they were born abroad or were raised abroad from a young age and do not know much about Iraq.

I do not seem to know many Iraqis my age. And certainly I do not know anyone my age with an experience similar to mine — except for my sister. I love and value all my friends. But I have a vastly different experience from my American friends, and from my Iraqi friends, and even from Iraqi relatives who are my age. My friends of my generation are few and very different from me. Hardly any of them had a similar experience of being away from their parents at a young age. They were always under the guidance of their parents. They settled down and had nice homes and families. They led a different life. Hardly any of them were there when we did our anti–Saddam activism in the 1980s and 1990s. When we did those events, everyone was older. My sister and I were the only teens.

* * *

It is rather amazing that the bold decision my parents made to take us kids — myself and my sister — out of Iraq at such a young age has brought such a profound experience on my life. Because I was detached from my parents at a young age, I did not have the Iraqi way of being looked after with every detail of my life as Iraqi youth are, and I therefore had no strong family presence in my daily life. In fact, I had no family involvement in my life. Typically in Iraq, as I mentioned before, youth are surrounded by care from their parents as well as from their extended family members. This was typical in Iraq then and still is now, but I did not have that experience. As I explained, my parents could not leave Iraq to stay with us. We spent some time in the United Kingdom before we came to the United States.

I went through important stages of my life without immediate family support and involvement and with only infrequent "long distance" guidance — on the phone — almost consultation-like and brief in nature from my parents and older siblings. Over a period of years I talked a few times to my parents when they could call us, but phone calls were restricted and also monitored by the Ba'ath government. It was much safer for them and us not to be in touch. This harsh experience required that I develop maturity and concentration as well as responsibility and resolve.

Because of that I feel that I have been independent and pioneering all my life. I am typically self-reliant in making my decisions and in executing them, and I do not expect anything from others. Maybe this is how I became patient and persevering. The best guidance I had was the rock-solid moral foundation that my parents laid in me when I was a kid by surrounding me with their love when I lived with them and even from afar. Other than that I hardly had much guidance or support. Of course my parents made sure that both my sister and I were safe with caring adults (our brothers), and thank God for that. Our brothers took basic care of us — made sure we were alive and breathing — but that's about it. They were not prepared to give us any guidance on most if not all issues of life. They were young, too — in their twenties. In fact maybe it was the other way around at times; maybe my sister and I gave guidance to them.

And interestingly, I also did not have the American way of absolute independence and freedom. Because of my Iraqi background and the strong foundation laid when I was a younger kid, I also kept my morals and values. I never touched any of the forbidden things such as alcohol, while this is the first thing many Arabs and Muslims do when they go to western countries.

This lack of a similar generational experience to mine — which I think had such a profound impact on me — has a few reasons. Not many families took their children (young like we were) abroad and especially not girls. This was a bold thing that my parents did. Let me explain that. There were Iraqi girls who went to study abroad in the 1970s and even in the 1960s, but that was different. These people went on a government sponsored program, and they were well looked after financially and to some degree even socially through the embassy. They were also allowed to contact their families regularly. I admire and salute those girls. In fact, my cousin is one of them. She studied in the United Kingdom in the

1960s. However, during that time that we left, no families were able to leave. Maybe individuals left, but not many families left. When my sister and I were in the U.K. or when we just came later to the U.S., most if not all of the friends we mingled with — say, Iraqis or Arabs — were older than us. Some were married and had children. So the people around us were either older than us or they were just babies and children. There was no one our age. This is important for me to explain because it has had a profound impact on my life. It made me jump from being a young teen to a responsible adult right away in one shot.

I hardly know anyone my age who left Iraq during those times. There are people my age who left Iraq much later than us — when they were in their twenties and thirties — and today there are many people who are leaving. But the story is rather different when you leave home as an adult. Add to that the fact that both of us, myself and my sister, started college right away in the United States, so we mingled more with people slightly older than us. However, these were school friends, and they were of various nationalities; some were Americans.

There are many things that one has to learn during the teenage years. I learned things as I went without much guidance from anyone. I had to do things in order to learn about them. To this day in Iraq, parents guide their children in everything from how to style their hair to how to fill out college entrance forms. And college education is free in Iraq (for the government sponsored universities, which are the majority of universities in Iraq), so they don't even have to worry about paying for their education. Young people in Iraq are very well looked after emotionally and economically. They are "raised" and reared for many years. Iraqi parents give immense help to their grown-up children in all steps of college life such as what field to study and where to study — which university, which city, and even their married life such as who to marry and where to live after you get married. Kids typically stay at home until they get married. Their parents provide for them throughout college, and their moms typically cook for them and even take care of their laundry until they leave home. Parents in Iraq look tenderly after their children. They guide them in every little step in life. Maybe only recently it has become common of men in their twenties to leave home and follow their job or education. But it is rare or impossible that a young unmarried woman would leave home and live by herself. The only exception to that is if she is going to university. In that case she would leave home during the university years and most likely stay with relatives or at the dorms.

I did not have any of that extended care and attention because I was far away from Mom and Dad. And because of all these aforementioned circumstances, being away from home and parents, not having much support, and going through important stages in my life quickly such as college and getting married, I feel my whole life has been rushed and all the important moments happened quickly in a very compressed way. In retrospect, I see how hard that was, but I made it through. By the time I was in my early and mid-twenties, I had done everything from college, to marriage to work to adjusting to living in the U.K. and then the U.S., to dealing with some health, school and marriage difficulties and the passing of both of my parents just a few months apart. For a couple of years initially I was living close to my sister and brother, but later we each went our own way, and actually they were as unprepared as I for most of the issues that I faced. I feel I have done so much and adjusted so quickly to many situations in a short period of time.

As a result of this experience, I like to do everything slowly. I feel that the only way for me to enjoy and appreciate things is if I do them slowly. I like to have my meals slowly. I like to read books slowly. If anything interests me I like to examine it and enjoy looking at it carefully and appreciatively or writing it down. And I feel that I must savor every second of my life and concentrate on everything and anything that I do, whether it is cooking, eating, washing the dishes, or something important such as talking to someone, reading a book, driving to work or opening a gift. I feel that I must enjoy these things slowly and capture their meaning or pleasure before they disappear and pass me by.

This is true even for life's serious things. Today I like to take decisions very slowly. I like to read and analyze everything from all angles and explore all options around me in a very cautious and nonspontaneous way. And further, I appreciate everything that I have, every opportunity, every friendship, every story, every new place, and I try to enjoy and benefit from any circumstance that I am in. I will never understand nor sympathize with anyone who whines about mediocre issues in life.

Because of my unusual life experience, few friends and relatives understand my plight and appreciate my journey. I appreciate and care for all my friends and relatives. However, I must mention one amazing lady, my friend Cristina. Not only do I love and admire her, but she truly understands me and appreciates all that I have done and still want to do. I am so lucky to have this wonderful lady in my life as a friend. She is closer to my age than my other friends and although she comes from far away — from Latin America — and we met and became friends in the United States, and although I am very far from her now because I am in Iraq, we are very close in ideas, inspirations, goals (we both have science careers), and tastes.

* * *

I feel that I stand as a witness and a link between generations of Iraqis and Iraqi Americans. If I did not write this book, a link between generations would be lost. I can understand both older and younger Iraqis. In Iraq, I still carry some of the older values that no one my age or younger seems to know or care about today, though the people older than me know very well. It is astounding that I — who spent my childhood in Iraq but have been away for three decades — know more about Iraqi values and culture than the Iraqi youth and kids of today who have always lived in Iraq. It is further astounding to me that I met some Iraqis who have recently emigrated out of Iraq, and when they come back to visit after one or two years they seem to have forgotten everything about Iraq. They keep saying how hard it is for them to adjust to living in the conditions of Iraq. In contrast, my husband and I, who have been away for many years, seemed to adjust okay — though of course with a lot of self-control and perseverance. For example, even though I have lived abroad most of my life, I still know the social norms in Iraq and I did not make any blunders (not yet!). I still can quickly adapt to most social situations as I did in many of the circumstances I have been through here in Iraq, although it was hard sometimes. Sometimes in various events the social norms take over and they rule and override all other things. For example, in meetings it is expected that older people take the lead in where they sit and choose their turn to speak, even though they may not be the most senior person professionally.

Not only do I stand between generations, I also stand between American and Iraqi cultures. I am a bridge between generations and between cultures. I am reaching out between Iraq and the United States. I bring those two worlds together. Here, too, I feel that if I had not written this book, another link across cultures and a beautiful truth would have been lost.

* * *

I learned beautiful things from living in the United States, and I want to take those things back to Iraq. I am a malleable link between these two worlds. I love telling people about the United States. I told my Iraqi friends and relatives about American food, American coffee, how we drive there, Thanksgiving, how we work, professionalism, being punctual, professional ethics and so on. I have also talked about the difficult side of American life, such as homeless people, guns and more.

And of course because much of my work deals with universities and science, I have told people about how amazing schools (universities) are in the U.S. I have talked about how we call universities "school"—it is not common to use this word in Iraq for university—and how standards are high, and what amazing facilities we have in the U.S. to do our scientific work and many other stories.

I also taught my Iraqi relatives and colleagues and even the students whom I met and who were departing for the U.S. for their studies many American expressions that are hard to translate and what their meaning is. For example:

How are you? I've been better.

You have the guts to ...

Thanks but no thanks

Push it under the rug

Let's call it a night

Play it by ear

I'll pass

He split

It takes two to tango

Music to my ears

Preaching to the choir

Actually, I must digress here and discuss something about the English language. There is a problem of poor translation from English to Arabic and vice-versa. This is true not only in Iraq but throughout the region. Lots of newspapers, travel related documents and even advertisements have many errors in translation. The correct way to translate, of course, is to convey the meaning and not just translate the words exactly. And further, text must be thought out in English in order for the translation to make sense. I saw many banners, forms, reports, and so on, all with very poor translation. In Iraq, this translation problem also pertains to various international aid organizations. The printed materials that the international organizations bring are poorly translated into Arabic so they do not make sense. The international organizations always make this mistake. Even when the materials they bring are good, they are not effective because of the poor translations.

Further, there is another problem that has arisen because of poor translation. Many TV channels air foreign programs, mostly English-language programs, that are translated via a subtitle printed at the bottom of the screen. Actually this too pertains to all the countries in the region, not just to Iraq. I have been to several nearby countries and I saw the same TV channels. First let me explain that in the Middle East most TV channels come via satellite. So they are aired to many countries simultaneously. No need for cable subscription. Typically, homes have access to some six or seven hundred TV channels of all sorts. All you need to buy is a receiver and some other piece of equipment that allows you to choose your channels and save them. And you can get more channels if you buy a different kind of receiver. Well, the movies and TV shows that come from the western countries come unedited for television display. That means all the bad language is there. The bad-language words are translated incorrectly and thus people think it's okay to say them and that they are just normal words. Even children began to use these words — and they don't even speak English — and no one stops them because the parents do not know that these are swear words in English. In fact one such case happened with an employee in one of the offices that I was in. He used some bad word in English in his conversation with someone. And it turned out that person's English was good and he was upset and made a complaint about the incident. The extent of poor translation is everywhere. Many times people use American expressions for work and business settings, and they translate them literally, and the outcome in Arabic makes no sense. Some memorable examples are "brainstorming," "thinking out loud," "astronomically high," and others. One day, my husband and I were listening to the weather forecast on TV. When the weather lady announced — in Arabic of course — that tomorrow the temperatures in several cities would be "trilateral numbers." We both asked each other, "What did she just say?" And then we burst out laughing. We figured they copied this expression from some American weather forecast that was perhaps referring to high temperatures in "triple digits."

On the other hand, Americans I have met in Iraq have learned some Iraqi habits and expressions. I think all Americans in Iraq know the word *inshallah,* which means "God willing." This expression is used by Iraqis and people in the region in general, regardless of their religion. It means we are planning to do something and we shall do it. But sometimes it can be misused to mean "We'll see." Also, most of the Americans I saw in Iraq have gotten used to having tea Iraqi style and having Turkish coffee — which is served in Iraq. It is kind of like espresso coffee, but it is blended with cardamom and usually served lightly sweetened, although it can also be served without sugar. It is somewhat softer and milder than espresso.

* * *

There are many amazing things about Americans and about the United States that I would like Iraqis to know about. There are things I would like Iraqis to learn to do. Over the years and through many experiences and friendships from my social interactions as well as work and a whole life that I have built in the U.S., I have come to admire specific American characteristics and behaviors, and I have learned many of these good qualities. If I were to describe Americans in a couple of words, I would have to say that they say what they mean and they are practical and humble people.

I very much admire how Americans accurately articulate their feelings and thoughts and how easily they express their emotions in words. Most people can tell you exactly how they feel and what they mean and what they want without much mumbo jumbo. They don't mind saying, "I am upset" or "I am sad" or "I am angry" or "I do not like your work" or "I do not agree with your ideas" — but they say it calmly and gently. Americans easily express how they feel and often ask one another, "How do you feel about this? I think this makes for healthy human relations and interactions. Also, it takes a lot of courage to talk about your problems.

IV. For Better or for Worse: Iraqis and Americans

Iraqis on the other hand do not openly express their feelings in words and do not talk much about feelings, although their feelings occupy a significant part of their lives. They may *act* as their feeling dictates, but they would not easily tell you how they feel. Iraqis are not direct in their communications. They tend to go around a subject and not hit it directly. For example, if you upset someone, they more likely would respond by being rude to you instead of telling you that they are mad at you. Alternatively and interestingly, if and when they talk about the emotions they feel — for example, if they know you very well — they talk about it in a dramatic, intense, and even graphic way. They actually overdramatize and deeply indulge in describing something that happened to them. But Iraqis would be reluctant to talk about their feelings on a talk show, especially if they were sad or had problems. I wish Iraqis would communicate directly and say exactly what they mean.

* * *

Americans are practical people with a get-things-done attitude. They tend to make things work efficiently and smoothly. This can be seen in many aspects of life, from organizing an event to completing a task. Whether the event is an important formal conference or a baby shower, it is well organized and runs smoothly. Everyone involved in an event does his or her task, no matter how small, and they do not think of it as insignificant. I very much like how things are done in steps and parts and things are completed one step and one segment at a time. I wish Iraqis would do things the same way.

Moreover, Americans are good at moving on after personal crises, whether illness or divorce or loss of something, or other tragedies that hit them. They grieve in private and after some time they try to collect themselves and what is left of their energy and decide it is time to move on. I understand from personal experience that some grieving never ends, and some wounds in our lives leave a scar in our soul and in our memory that never goes away, but there is a moment when one decides to move on and get on with one's life while not necessarily forgetting the crisis. Iraqis, in general, do not move on easily. They continue to mourn a personal crisis such as a divorce or the loss of personal property. I have met Iraqis who talk intensely about an event or an accident that happened to them years before and they still hurt over it. They talk about it in a mourning way

155

and never seem to move on. It is hard to move on, and of course I know that this varies by individuals, too. It depends on many factors, such as the prospects one has for moving on and how important one's loss was.

I also have come to admire how Americans take care of a disabled child or sibling. I have seen such stories on television and have met a couple such families. They show them love, respect their humanity, and accept their imperfect bodies and accept them as they are. That is admirable. I do not think we in Iraq have come near that level of dedication. We tend to hide away our imperfect children and we do not treat them as well. In fact I can say that I never saw handicapped children when I lived in Iraq as a child because simply no one took them out. You never saw them then. I think this attitude has changed over the recent years. And I think perhaps also recently there are more services available for handicapped people outside so that they can actually go out. And I did learn during my current stay in Iraq that there are indeed schools for such kids, and actually this issue has gained significance even in the current plans for education and rehabilitation projects. Further, because of three decades of wars, there are many handicapped men, young and old, and many maimed people of all ages because of terrorist attacks. We need to learn from Americans how to provide services for these dear people and how to care for our handicapped children.

* * *

What I also like very much is that Americans work hard and play hard. Put differently, they do things at their time. At work they are serious and do all that it takes to do a job correctly. I am very proud to have learned this and to practice it in my work life. Many people in the United States work very hard, working long hours, sometimes starting at 4 or 5 A.M. Some of them must travel long distances to reach their work, around an hour or more. Some Americans work two jobs or they have a job and go to school (university). And some people have kids and no one to support them with raising their kids.

At the same time, when it is time for fun and celebrations, Americans also do a good job. And the time of celebrations is just that: *for celebrations*. It is rare that Americans talk about work details at a social or celebratory event — although there are exceptions. But in general they save work for work.

* * *

There is a salient different between Iraqis and Americans, especially the youth, that is very striking. Given that Iraqis have witnessed many wars, crises and injustices in recent years, one would expect them to be tough as persons, but they are not. In spite of the wars and turbulence of recent times, Iraqis remain tender — in a positive way — as individuals, as if the crises did not go through us. Iraqis take it to heart too much if something minor happens to them. They talk about it in a dramatic, exaggerated way. And when you listen carefully, you see it is a minor issue. There is a general softness and tenderness about Iraqis which comes close to naïveté. This is also tied to the fact that most Iraqis live at home well into their twenties and even sometimes their thirties, as I mentioned before. Youth are protected and guided by their families even as adults. They are not well experienced in life. It is common to see people living at home as adults and being still cared for in some ways by their parents. For example, women still look after their grown-up children — who are in university — on a daily basis, perhaps cooking for them and tending to their daily activities.

Likewise in spite of the relative ease of life that Americans have — at least with regard to political stability and lack of recent wars on their home soil — one would expect Americans to be soft and malleable. But they are not. They are tough — in a positive way — and strong spirited and handle crises in a practical way, even as they give grief its own space and time. Most Americans leave home very early in their lives, and it is rare to see them still living with parents beyond their early twenties. They tend to split off the family early and have their own independent lives. American youth do amazing things at an early age — for example, internships. I tried to explain this concept to Iraqis, but they do not see why would anyone do an internship and not get paid. They do not see the importance of contacts, networking, mentoring , experience, and simply how exciting an internship can be. When I tell people, "You are still young, you can work any job! It does not have to come with high pay and high prestige — this is how you build you career!" they do not accept it.

* * *

It is easy to be yourself among Americans. They are humble. You do not have to pretend anything because Americans are really good at

157

accepting people the way they are. Americans do not argue to prove that you are wrong. For the most part, they mind their own business. For example, I have had more acceptance from many American friends, who come from different walks of life, about my Muslim dress and the fact that I do not drink than what I have had from some Muslim and even from some Iraqi friends. I have attended many social parties, weddings and other events in the United States with my Muslim "veil" and I did not drink alcohol and never had a problem or an insult from anyone. If they talk about it, it is out of curiosity and interest and rarely is it judgmental. But when you go with "high life" Iraqis you hear all sorts of comments about the veil. We Iraqis are more picky and judgmental at times.

There are things about the United States that most Iraqis do not know and that I would like to tell them. Most Iraqis think of the United States as crowded big cities with skyscrapers and rush hour traffic. They do not know much about the strikingly beautiful nature in America. I was the same way before I came to the U.S. Certainly there are stunning buildings, and I personally love downtown buildings and city styles. When I first came to the U.S., I was not that interested in nature and was not particularly looking for any special natural scenery. But after seeing some areas of the United States, even I who am not a nature fan was amazed and excited by the beautiful nature scenes. Perhaps also age has something to do with that. Maybe when I was younger, I did not appreciate nature that much.

Not many things I have done have been more enchanting and more magical than driving across the desert at night, all the way from southern California to the Grand Canyon in Arizona. The long ride across the desert is overwhelming to many, perhaps, but every moment of it is rather pleasurable for those who love adventure and intensity. As you roll along interstate highway I-40 East at night cutting through the daunting darkness of the surrounding desert, the sky — in contrast — brightly glitters with hundreds of thousands of stars as if it were a velvet drape embroidered with pearls and diamonds ready for a big celebration in the heavens. Miles and miles of driving under this glistening sparkle showed us scenes so captivating that we — my husband and I — stopped the car to gaze at the sky, amazed and excited at this magnificent and unforgettable beauty.

I am definitely a city person. I love big cities and don't mind their traffic and pollution. I just love to see the crowds hurrying around. I even love the feeling you have when you search for parking, and I like the noise of big cities. I spent most of my time in the U.S. in Los Angeles, an incredibly beautiful and stirring place. I loved everything in L.A. and everything about it: its sophisticated culture, amazing cuisine, diversity, and endless excitement and the wonderful friends I have there. I even loved the traffic jams, being stuck on the 405 freeway, the noise, down-town and the crowded areas. But I also love L.A. because it resembles Baghdad in many ways — or at least what Baghdad used to be decades ago when I spent my childhood there. First, the dry weather is definitely very similar to that in Baghdad in the spring and summer. In addition, some of the long stretching roads in the "inland empire" resemble those in Baghdad. There were several posh areas in Baghdad — such as the well known Almansour, where I lived before — with homes similar to and even more beautiful than those of Beverly Hills and Bel Air, and several crowded cool areas similar to the Santa Monica promenade and Pasadena.

As awed as I was by the starry skies of the desert, I was even more amazed when we finally visited the Grand Canyon around midday. The beauty of that part of earth is beyond what words can describe. As if the starry skies of the night were not captivating enough, I was even more taken by the dazzling colors of the rocks and sand in amazing variations of copper and gold colors under the intense sun of the western United States, from the Grand Canyon and Bryce Canyon to Lake Powel in Utah.

The beauty of nature in the United States is not only in the West but throughout the vast land. The fall season in the Northeastern and Midwestern parts of the United States is magnificent, as I mentioned earlier. During the first few years that I was in the United States, I lived in Ohio, and I frequently traveled by car around the northeastern areas and saw the beautifully colored fall leaves. I was so amused and taken by these leaves that I used to collect them and use them as decorations at home. More than two decades later I returned to those areas and drove around just to see the fall colors again. It is like being in a magical world where the trees are not green but amazing shades of red, pink, gold and yellow.

The sky too takes on amazing colors in the United States. The col-orful sunsets in Florida can be a fiery orange or have soft shades of pink and lavender. The sunrise is even more powerful and more inspiring. Yet when the storms hit the whole sky gets draped with a dramatic grey shade and the water loses its turquoise color and blends with the grey clouds. The intensely forceful winds shake and bend the trees. Amidst this intensity one can hear the gentle whisper as the peaceful branches respond to the feisty winds during the night. The dramatic weather in Florida is deeply stirring to the mood.

Even more dazzling colors can be seen during lightning storms in the spring and summer as you are driving across open fields in the Midwest. Across the fields and plains one can see such dramatically beautiful colors of the sky during lightning. It is like the whole world turns purple and brilliant blue momentarily. It is so exciting to see, and I still love it.

* * *

One thing available in the U.S. that I would really like to have in Iraq is restaurants that are open all the time. I really enjoy restaurants and shops that are open 24 hours a day. There was nothing like that in Iraq, and when I first went to the United States, that was a new thing for me. And even more amazing is that these restaurants served breakfast any time and all the time. That was fun and luxurious and a nice treat in the middle of the night when you are in the mood to go out. It is not really just about food, but rather about the freedom to go out and eat breakfast at odd times. It gave me a sense of freedom and nonconformity to see people awake at night and going on with their lives at unusual times. Of course I do realize that some customers who go there do not go for fun but because they work night shifts or may be traveling on the road and need a meal and so on. But I do like to go out in the middle of the night and eat breakfast. Nowadays I know there are many such places in many countries. I think we will not have them in Iraq for a while, because there is no culture of eating out in the middle of the night as such. I do not really know what people who work late — such as doctors or truck drivers or taxis drivers — do about their meals in Iraq.

I did try to introduce some American culture in Iraq — bit by bit. I invited people over for breakfast. This was a new idea, because no one does that in Iraq. And while a few people really appreciated and enjoyed it, others found it a bit odd.

Actually, breakfast is my favorite meal, and no one does breakfast better than Americans. I think breakfast is a serious meal in American culture, while in Iraq breakfast is usually light or even nonexistent. For Iraqis, lunch is the main meal of the day.

I like the American style breakfast — all of it. The biscuits, the pastries, the pancakes, the (American) "French" toast, and of course the continuous coffee. On a trip to Asia a few years back, my husband and I stayed at an American hotel chain. Being in Asia and taking a local approach to breakfast, the hotel was catering to the local population, so they served noodles, meat and rice and other things at the main breakfast area. We could not eat these items for breakfast. We kept looking until we found the real American breakfast that we are used to: the pancakes, the cereal, and so on.

Over the years I even learned that you can have business meetings over breakfast or even invite people over for breakfast — or brunch — something which I like to do very much and perhaps I will try at my office one day. And of course no discussion about Americans is complete without talking about coffee or "American coffee" as it is known throughout the world wherever I have traveled. As much as Iraqis drink tea, Americans drink coffee, pretty much all day long. Americans serve coffee everywhere. At home nearly everyone has a "coffee maker," which only Americans use. Nearly all work places, no matter how small, have a corner set up for making coffee, and when you go to places such as banks, agencies, and real estate offices, usually you will be served coffee. Even at some gas stations and rest areas they just give free coffee to any passerby, though of course nowadays, with the economic crisis, some places have cut these services down.

Not only do Americans serve coffee everywhere, but most restaurants serve coffee endlessly — that is, they keep refilling your cup. Moreover, many Americans have a habit of stopping at some coffee shop to get coffee before they go to work. Most of these cafés and coffee shops open rather early, perhaps at five or six in the morning, to catch the business of those of us who love to stop and get coffee and take it with them. I am one of those people. This is very American and not many people understand that.

Recently I was in the Gulf region, and getting coffee in the morning presented a problem. Although these Gulf countries have nearly all the American and European food chains, and they have them in multiples within a small perimeter, the local Arab culture is such that these shops do not open until 10 or 11 A.M. It was impossible to get coffee in the morning. The one coffee stand on campus (where I worked) that made some interesting coffees opened at seven thirty, and I used to go there around quarter to eight to get coffee before my class, but that did not work either. I was told the machines had not heated up properly by that time and I would have to wait some twenty minutes, and of course I could not because I had to go to work. Of course Iraqis reading this might say: What's the big deal? Just make coffee at home. Of course I could make coffee at home, but it is not the same. I can't really explain it. It is not just about coffee; it is about socializing, talking, sharing ideas and brain-storming over business proposals and even scientific concepts — as I have done many times with my colleagues throughout the years in the United States. I really do not know if this is the right explanation. It is something that Americans just do.

For a while, I ended up buying some ready-to-use packs of coffee from the United States and taking them with me when I traveled back and forth. Interestingly, months later in the city of Alain in the United Arab Emirates where I stayed for a while, there was one coffee shop that, upon demand from all the Americans who lived there, started opening at 6 A.M. I was elated. When I went there in the morning around seven before work I saw all the Americans getting their "American" coffee — and pastries too.

* * *

I was surprised by the style of the young people whom I met at school in Ohio at Owens College and the University of Akron. They were all dressed casually, mostly in jeans or similar casual clothes. Although I had never been to any university in Iraq, I knew from my relatives that university students dressed up formally. Actually, they had to wear a uniform, but they chose their uniform pieces rather carefully. The women typically wore high heels, makeup and jewelry and wore their hair in many interesting ways. The men chose their ties and jackets meticulously. No one would come to university in casual clothes or regular outfits. University was the first stage of semi-independence for young people in Iraq, and although they had to wear a uniform they made the most out of it and wore nice clothes.

In the United States, where universities do not impose uniforms and students can wear whatever they please, most students came to their classes in casual clothes, wore their hair very simply, and in the summer most of them wore shorts, simple tops and slippers. This was very shocking to me. In Iraq, university is a formal place. No one would ever wear slippers to university. Another astonishing thing was to see professors in university dressed casually, without a suit or tie. In the summer they might even show up in shorts! That was very surprising to me then and would still surprise many Iraqis today. Professors in Iraq dress up formally. And I am sure that equally shocking to all Americans would be how much gold Iraqi women and girls put on, even at work, on a daily basis.

Americans tend to dress casually most of the time. I think they seek comfort more than the look in clothes. Most Americans would not dress up unless they had a formal business meeting or social event. Further, I am equally amazed at the simplicity of wedding dresses and bridal makeup here in the U.S. These are extremely simple compared to those in Iraq and in Arab cultures in general. I have attended many weddings in the United States over the years for American friends. All of the weddings were very beautiful and memorable, and I have noticed that the bridal dresses tend to be beautiful but plain — not overly ornamented — and the bride's makeup is soft and kept to a minimum. I have also looked at bridal fashion magazines and noticed the same thing.

In Iraq and the Middle East in general, the bridal dresses are so complicated and heavily ornamented and the makeup of the bride is so intense that sometimes you can barely see her. Although these ornaments can be exquisite and gorgeous, to people in the U.S. they might seem to be too much. Also, it is very normal for the bride and other women at weddings and other parties in the U.S. to wear their hair down. In Iraq, women must put their hair up in some exquisite sophisticated hairdo that must be professionally done at the hair salon. Rarely does a woman go to a party wearing her hair down. It usually means that she could not or did not go to the hair salon.

* * *

Americans prepare and eat vegetables in an entirely different way than Iraqis do. Although I mentioned in the previous sections that Iraqis serve and eat fruits twice or three times a day and they serve enormous amounts of fruits, Iraqis hardly eat vegetables and hardly ever serve them uncooked. Mostly, vegetables are served cooked within a stew or in a complicated but very delicious dish called *dolma* which includes many stuffed vegetables such as zucchini, onion, bell peppers and grape leaves. No one serves carrots or asparagus just slightly cooked or even uncooked as we do in the U.S. (which I like very much and serve most of the time). When I serve such vegetables to many Iraqi friends or relatives they are surprised by it and most of the times no one eats them.

Iraqis do eat salad, pretty much standard like any other salad, but they would be surprised if the fruits and vegetables in salad were not peeled. Also Iraqis cut the ingredients for salad much smaller than Americans do. If you were to prepare your salad with large pieces of tomato or cucumber, it would not be well received in Iraq.

The best salads I have ever had were in Los Angeles. Restaurants in L.A. serve the most unusual salads prepared in the most creative ways. Adding fruits and nuts to your standard salad and serving it in the most colorful oddly shaped plates gives one a sensational dining experience. I have prepared such salads for my Iraqi and Arab friends and relatives and my salads always stir up discussion. California cuisine is one of the things I love most, and I try to follow it when I prepare meals. In general, however, Iraqis are not courageous when it comes to trying new dishes and new recipes. They are dogmatic in their menus, as I mentioned before. They like to serve their traditional foods. If you make new, interesting dishes, it is likely that not many people will try them. And as I said earlier, Iraqis are too proud of their food. They do not like other foods very much. I think Americans are more at ease trying different cuisines. In fact a funny thing happened to me with some Iraqi friends. We had invited some friends over for breakfast. And I assumed that everyone was like us — interested in American-style breakfast. I prepared muffins, rolls, a fruit platter, eggs and some Arabic-style bread with cheese. In addition my husband prepared a platter of Iraqi-style cheese. During the breakfast, hardly anyone touched the rolls, muffins and fruit platter. Nearly everyone ate the traditional cheese and the Arabic bread. I ended up with a lot of muffins stored in my freezer.

* * *

Unlike Iraqis, Americans are informal with each other. They call people by their first names. Iraqis prefer to use titles. They use the words "sir" and "Mr." and "Dr." often, sometimes not even in the appropriate place. People hardly speak to each other without a title unless it is within a family. That is not the case in the United States. In my biology lab at university, having just recently come from Iraq, I addressed my T.A. as "sir." That is a normal Iraqi thing because teachers and professors and T.A.s are highly revered and respected in Iraq. My T.A. was very surprised and told me, "You don't have to call me sir, you can just call me Dave." It became apparent to me over the years of school that academic environments in the U.S., in spite of their brilliant high standards scientifically and intellectually, are more relaxed than they are in Iraq. American universities provide an atmosphere of academic freedom and excellence in education. Professors are engaged in their research and teaching and are judged by their intellect and excellence, not their political or religious affiliations. In Ba'athist Iraq, loyalty to the government was the most important measure of performance.

* * *

Interestingly, Iraqis and even Arabs in general think of the United States — and even other western countries — as being violent societies. When they say that, they are usually referring to crimes such as shootouts, rapes, and gang activity, which seem to occur at higher rates in the West. Iraqis wonder why there should be that much crime in the West, given the excellent living conditions, the political stability and freedom and the access to police protection? Actually I do not know the answer, and I leave that to sociologists to make such analyses. But there are indeed too many crimes in the U.S.: burglaries, homicides, rapes and serial murders. However, in the U.S. they talk about these things in detail and in depth. And this is really important. In the U.S., society deals openly with such issues and experts figure out their causes, and how to avoid them, how to deal with them after they happen. And this is good.

In the early 1980s when I first came to America, it was intensely shocking to me to learn about people getting stabbed and even killed in burglary-driven crimes such as bank robberies and customers taken hostage or people being mugged and other crimes that seemed to dominate the local news. Of course there were burglaries even in Iraq a long time ago when I was there, but no one would stab or shoot over stealing money or some item.

But more disturbing were the crimes of serial killers. The local news talked about them and the gruesome nature of these complex crimes in detail. It was also shocking to me that people could buy guns and carry them or keep them at home and that many homes in the United States have guns. Often I heard on the news about little children who accidentally used these guns and harmed themselves or someone in the family.

Also surprising and new to me were all the tips and information on how to walk safely and protect yourself in vulnerable situations. I had never thought about these things before. In Iraq there were not that many crimes and murders that we knew about. Most of the violence we experienced as a society was at the hand of the government. The Ba'ath regime terrorized us as a society. Saying the words Ba'ath, Alamin, or Almukhabrart to any Iraqi would bring back many bad memories from Saddam's regime. But as a society, in Iraq we did not have high levels of crime. Of course there were crimes, but not as much and not as gruesome as those of the serial killers of the 1980s that I learned about in the U.S.

I learned later over the years that in the U.S. crimes are reported and statistics are kept properly and that is why we hear about them a lot. In the U.S. it is admirable how they report these things correctly and lay them out so that problems can be dealt with. And there are many impartial agencies which do such reporting. This is something good that I wish Iraqis and Arabs in general would learn from Americans. The general trend in Iraq and other Arab countries is that you do not report and do not make public such problems. You tend to not bring too much attention to them — although this has changed in recent years and there are many reports out and even discussions on television and in conferences. Nevertheless, from the first few months we lived in the U.S., my sister and I began to learn safety tips. We walked vigilantly and attentively, and we did not carry too much cash.

Throughout the 1980s also there were a series of crimes in the United States involving tampering with food products. There was a problem with tainted baby food, and someone tainted Tylenol with cyanide. These crimes were very much in the news and discussed at length during those days. It was the first time in my life to learn of such a crime. Who would think of tampering with baby food? For me as someone who had just come to the United States, this type of crime was strange and I had never heard of such a thing. But I also remember very well that after those incidents the manufacturing companies became vigilant in their safety technologies, and food and medications were packaged in ways that was difficult to tamper with. I like how Americans learn from bad experiences and take corrective steps.

In recent years, new violent phenomena have arisen in the U.S., things that I did not see in the 1980s. Random massive shootouts have occurred in schools, at post offices, and even on freeways as drive-by shootings. Each of those events shocked Americans, including me. These seem to have become more common in recent years. And I have heard many discussions on television and in various forums about kids having guns at schools and schools having to employ security and police and even to utilize metal detectors.

I followed these cases with great interest. These types of crimes for the most part were done by deranged individuals. However, in nearly all these cases — as we follow these stories in the media — the criminals "seemed normal" on a daily basis to their friends, neighbors and peers. And it is fair to say that some of them were deranged but others were just acting out their personal frustrations with life. This issue was of interest to me and still is.

Although one assumes in general that poverty breeds crime, and it is probably true in many cases, Iraq did not have such high level of crime when I lived there as a child. I think that the high personal discipline linked to high moral values, strict social norms and the high regard placed on the family in Iraq is what protected Iraqis from violence. In spite of the poverty and harsh totalitarian conditions throughout the 1980s and 1990s, Iraqis did not have such violence. The immense violence that erupted around 2004–2007 was, as I mentioned before, brought from outside and thrived in Iraq and had political motivations.

* * *

Most Iraqis incorrectly assume that all Americans live the high life, that everyone has a lot of luxuries and lives a life like those shown in American movies. Well, many Americans indeed do. For some, material success is the "American Dream." Many people attach their happiness and their standard of success to achieving this level of comfortable life.

But even for the average person, life is not bad because there are services available that make life rather easy. For example you can order things by mail; you can expect the bus to arrive on time; all cities have basic services such as clean water and police service; most companies will refund your money if they did not deliver a service; there are shops open twenty four hours; and so on. But Iraqis do not know how hard most Americans work. They work two jobs, they work and go to school, they drive long distances to go to their jobs, and so on.

* * *

Most Iraqis think that Americans are liberal and nonreligious. And I too thought that when I first came to the U.S. To my surprise, I met many young people who took religion very seriously and who attended Bible study at university. And later over the years I also met many adults and families who were religious. There are religious schools, religious summer camps, religious scientific societies and even missionaries. I was approached by missionaries a few times over the years. Moreover, I was also surprised to know that there was organized religion and even fundamentalists in the United States.

Iraqis have heard that in the United States there is separation between church and state, and most interpret that to mean that religion has no role in politics in the United States. This is wrong. What it really means is that churches and other religious entities operate freely without supervision or dictation from the government. In most Muslim countries, on the other hand, governments interfere in what religious leaders can or cannot say or do. In some "moderate" Gulf countries, the government distributes a script each week to all the mosques and the Imam of the mosque (the imam is like the priest of the church) *must* use the script for his speech or sermon. He is not allowed to make his own speech!

Most liberal Muslims in Iraq and elsewhere in the Arab world use the western idea of separation between church and state as their basic argument for subduing religion. They confuse being religiously neutral (irreligious, religiously tolerant) with being anti-religion and persecuting religion. They think that separation of religion from politics means the absence of religion and that automatically means liberalization of society. Most Iraqis do not know that religion actually has a very strong role in politics in the United States, and usually it brings conservatism to politics.

Religion affects many of life's areas in the United States. For example, health issues that the government regulates, such as abortion and euthanasia, are religiously polarizing. Religious beliefs and personal conduct of political candidates are subject to high scrutiny by the public in all elections. Even educational issues, such as whether schools may teach evolution and sex education, have polarized communities based on religion. Those who are conservative do not want their children to learn about evolution and do not want them to have explicit sex education. They believe that it is their role to teach appropriate behaviors based on their values. The United States constitution forbids the establishment of any religion by the government, but religion is important in the United States.

Americans are interested in many religions, but when I first came to the United States in the 1980s, not many Americans seemed to recognize Muslim dress. At that time, not many Muslim women or girls in America put on the veil. My sister and I, however, wore our Muslim dress in the United States. And interestingly, many Americans thought that I was a nun. I was asked, "Are you a nun?" or "What order are you?" many times when I lived in Ohio. And because my sister and I often walked together and we used to buy identical clothes when we were younger, we provoked even more such friendly curiosity. I did not mind these inquires. I was happy to answer people.

* * *

In Iraq the common stereotype of American women is that they are all are liberal and liberated, so I was surprised when I discovered that many American women are stay-at-home moms. Iraqis tend to think that all western women, and especially American women, work outside of the home and abandon their motherly duties and that this is a sign of freedom and liberation. It is not true. I think the majority of American women do take good care of their kids, and the majority who are working do so because of economic reasons: They need the money. But I know of many American women who chose to stay home until their kids were grown, and some put their careers on hold for many years.

In Iraq, having children is not a problem for a working woman; the entire extended family usually automatically helps the woman to care for her children while she is at work. It is a given. And in this regard, it is much easier for working women in Iraq than for their peers in the U.S.

And also, there are other options in Iraq for childcare, such as preschool and in-home servants who also care for the children. And women who are employees of the public sector can have a maternity leave of up to one year, and their job is protected and waits for them when they decide to come back! Nice perk indeed.

But even more surprising to me about American women was the fact that most American women who are married change their last name to that of their husband. This did not fit my stereotype of the "liberated" American woman. Married women in Iraq almost always keep their own family name and do not take their husband's name.

And one more thing on names: Iraqis use their first name, their father's name and their last name (which usually is a family name). The use of a "middle" name in the U.S. is not easily understood by Iraqis. Why do we need a middle name? I do not know the answer to that. But because all application forms here in the U.S. have an area for middle name, most Iraqis who come to the U.S. end up using their father's name as a middle name. In Iraq, the Ba'ath regime instituted a policy by which the use of family names became illegal. So most Iraqis who were born during that era do not have their family name listed on their documents — just their first name, father's name and grandfather's name.

I like to add two other observations about how Iraqi women are different from their counterparts in the U.S. First, older women in Iraq are much more active, vibrant, and highly involved in the daily matters of their families, including continuing to "raise" their grown-up children and babysitting their grandchildren. Many times they live with the family of their son or daughter. This makes them busy and involved. I am sure it gives them less independence and privacy, but it keeps them more or less happy and busy. Further, you always see older women in the holy shrines, going there with their friends. You can see that they are occupied mentally with many issues. All in all, older women in Iraq are engaged with family and community. Therefore, old age–related emotional and cognitive decline, as seen in Alzheimer's disease, dementia or depression, are not common in Iraq.

When I went to the holy shrines, the visiting areas were separate for men and women. The shrines are very crowded, but you would be surprised how well many older women manage their way in the crowds. In fact when I went there I found it quite physically challenging, even though I am rather fit — I exercise and jog and sometimes lift weights. I was pushed and pulled among the crowds. Older women seem to be physically strong and happy in spite of the immense suffering their society has been through.

My other observation, and this is not just in Iraq but in many countries in the Middle East and especially in the Gulf region and in Iraq, is that unmarried women and married women are quite distinct and behave differently. This is not the case in the West, where there is no apparent difference in the conduct or appearance of a married woman and a single woman. In the U.S. and in the West in general, married women, non-married women and teenage girls all try to look sexy and attractive. They all wear the same things, more or less; they do their hair, their nails, and so on.

In the Middle East there is really no such thing as young women who are dating — or at least they are very unusual. Relations with men are still limited to marriage, for the most part. I do not mean to be old-fashioned and I do realize things have changed even in Iraq, but for the most part, relations with men are only through marriage. I mention this matter because it is reflected in how girls, married women, and non-married women look and behave. Although (as I mentioned before) Iraqi females of all ages wear excessive quantities of gold regardless of their marital status, these three groups of females are otherwise different in their clothing style, conversations and body language. Married women are not that flashy in their style and tend to be more conservative. They take too much pride in, and give too much attention to, their daughters. Young women are spoiled, and in well-to-do families they are very well provided for as far clothes and jewelry. Younger non-married girls and older non-married women are more flashy and perhaps less conservative.

When you visit a lingerie store you mostly find married women (and men) buying lingerie. You hardly see unmarried single females going to these stores alone (though they may go with a female relative). What's really very odd in Iraq is that most lingerie stores are staffed by men. I noticed that the few times that I did go out into the shops. I haven't the slightest idea why it is so and how women can look and choose lingerie comfortably with males assisting them!

* * *

The concept of marriage seems to be a bit softer and wider in the United States. By softer I mean marriage can be easily terminated and many people go through divorce. By wider I mean marriage encompasses many nontraditional marriages, such as people getting married and divorced a few times or getting remarried at a much older age such as in their fifties. In general, Americans get married much later in age than Iraqis do. In the United States, there are no stigmas attached to being single, divorced or remarried for the third time. People tend to assess the marriage in how it is serving their lives and terminate it if they wanted to. They are indeed practical; if the marriage is impeding their happiness or goals, they terminate it. (Of course I know not all Americans accept divorce.) In Iraq the concept of marriage is more classical and people usually do not remarry many times. That would be considered unusual in Iraq, especially for women. And although divorce in Iraq has caught up with other countries — meaning there is more divorce today than before — it remains difficult to obtain a divorce and most families would discourage it unless there were serious circumstances.

The lives of married couples in the United States give more time to the couple themselves. It's normal for a couple to do things on their own without their kids. I think this is nice. I think Iraqi couples' lives are more like a long journey, focusing mainly on the children's lives and having much less time for themselves — until their grown-up children get married, after which they might do all sorts of interesting stuff together such as going on trips and especially going on the Hajj (the Muslim pilgrimage). Also, in the U.S. we tend to accept families with adopted children, children from other marriages and couples without children much more than we do in Iraq. Not having children myself, I was subjected to traumatizing questions and comments throughout many years — while I lived in the U.S. and even now — mostly from my Iraqi and Arab friends and even just from acquaintances and some relatives.

One more thing on marriage. The concept of a "bridal registry" would be highly unusual to all Iraqis. It took me many years to figure it out, and I am still not used to it. I explained it to many people I know in Iraq. But actually, for all the weddings that I attended in the United States, I never used this system and I always took my own gifts. I just like that my gifts express my own taste and my impression of the people receiving the gift. Also "bridal showers" are new to all Iraqis. There is no equivalent to that in Iraq. Maybe the closest thing I could think of is the henna party, where someone comes to adorn the hands of the bride-to-be with henna. Of course there is also food and music. Also there is a unique tradition that some female relatives of the bride and the groom assist her in buying her constellation of dresses and accessories that she will wear during the several parties that will take place.

Iraqis also do not have the custom of sending a "thank you" card after receiving a gift or after having a visit with someone as Americans do. They express their gratitude verbally when they receive the gift and after they use it, or they reciprocate the gesture by presenting another gift. Or they use the gift in front of the person who gave it to them — for example, they wear a dress or a perfume that they received from someone in that person's presence.

Sending cards on various occasions is a very American thing to do. I like it. I have a big collection of cards from various family and friends and co-workers that I have had for many years. Iraqis give cards only occasionally.

* * *

Iraqis and Americans

The American troops have left as I write these words in the very last days of December 2011. The winter in Baghdad was unusually mild,[1] and I think that eased the tension of the much talked about troop withdrawal. At least the weather did not exacerbate the situation. However, the same period was marked by a sudden eruption of defiance among political groups, accompanied by a new wave of terrorist attacks, some of which were close to us in the IZ. It was loud, and the glass in the hallway outside my room was shattered. There were tanks and military vehicles all over the IZ. It was like going back to square one instead of moving forward. And some seven months later, that saga is still ongoing. It goes on and on to the point that ordinary people have become tired of talking about the political parties — what they want, what they mean, what would it take to for them to make up. People are also tired of trying to figure out the new political parties that split from the major ones and who is on whose side.

* * *

But where are Iraqis and Americans headed? The Iraq war and the events that followed have impacted and continue to impact the lives of all Americans and all Iraqis in powerful ways. Both Iraq and the United States are bound by the consequences of the 2003 war for decades to come. Both of our societies have been deeply shaken by the war and will continue to be affected for generations. Iraq became a household name and will be with Americans in our daily conversations for decades to come. It will be in our textbooks and on future application forms indicating a person's war veteran status. The word *Alamrecan*, which means "Americans," has become common in every conversation all over Iraq, in topics ranging from the security procedures to fixing the electric power to real estate prices in Baghdad. Future generations in both countries will always have something to say about the war that touched them personally.

Thousands of Americans have lost their sons and daughters in this war or have been physically or psychologically injured in combat or by traumatic loss of family members and even loss of their normal self. The U.S. economy has been damaged by the war. Every American household has been affected by Iraq. Similarly, millions of Iraqis have felt the impact of the war in similar or even more devastating ways. Millions of Iraqis, too, have been affected by death in their families, crippling injuries, loss of homes, displacement from homes, exposure to crime and mafias, terrorism, and — sadly for all Iraqi children — the traumatic effects of experiencing war. Everyone in Iraq will have something personal to say about this war. The impact of the war on Iraqis is even larger than on Americans, because Iraq is a smaller country and because the war has been fought on Iraqi soil.

The impact of the events of the past nine or so years on our lives is not going to disappear. It is going to be with us for a long time. Since the lives of Iraqis and Americans have been intermingled and since we have a long way to go together, a long time during which we will have an impact on each other, it is necessary to look towards the future and seek understanding of each other. This understanding is not a luxury, and it is not too late to achieve it. We need it for several reasons.

First, we need it for our own sake because our long journey ahead together is leading us to a place called the future. In order to make that future livable and the path towards it endurable, we must all know who we are traveling with, what those people are all about, and how to communicate with them.

Second, hundreds of thousands of families, both in Iraq and in the United States, have been directly affected if not devastated by the war. They are living with loss, pain and agony on a daily basis. I would like us all to stop and think about that. Just on that sentence alone, I could write a thousand books. This is no easy sacrifice. The story of each individual, whether American or Iraqi, who was killed, maimed, injured, widowed, orphaned, traumatized by the smell of death, or terrified by the sound of explosions, is important and should be documented and heard. The story of each person should be cherished, protected and respected. And for the rest of us, those stories should be an inspiration to help others and to do something that takes our societies towards healing. People's lives have changed during these years of war. Their happiness has gone. Their life journeys have been marred. They gave up precious parts of their existence and it is for them that we must examine where we are headed and how we are going to make it work. We must have some good outcome for Iraqis and for Americans after all these sacrifices.

I want to help Americans understand Iraq and Iraqis understand the United States. I stand between these two countries that I love and that have given me so much, and I feel obligated to put things right for them and between them and enable our two societies to move forward in spite of our pain and our losses.

Not many people have had both Iraq and the United States shape their lives. I have. Not many people love Iraq and the United States. I do. Both Iraq and the United States are part of who I am. As I breathed the air and drank the water in the United States for nearly three decades, my Iraqi roots grew beautifully in American soil. I know American values and I care about them, and I know Iraqi values and I care about them I learned fundamental principles of life from both countries. I spent my childhood in Iraq until I was fourteen, and I spent my teenage and all my adult life in the United States. I relate to both cultures and I know both cultures very well. In my attempt to increase understanding between the two, I hope I have corrected some stereotypes that Americans have about Iraqis and vice-versa.

175

I am grateful to both of those great countries for my belonging to them. It is in Iraq that I spent the most important years of my childhood and where I, like children everywhere, learned from my family and environs basic and fundamental values and where the red lines are drawn. And it is in the United States, where I have been throughout my adult life, that I learned everything else that I know, where I had the best education, where I was exposed to the best professional environment, and where I did all the important things of my adult life such as working, voting, and getting married. And most importantly, it is in the United States where I experienced freedom: freedom to speak and think as I wish, and freedom to criticize government officials and hold them accountable through voicing my opinion and participating in politics. This is something unheard of throughout the Arab world — at least until the Arab Spring events of the past year or so — and was especially unthinkable in Iraq. In Ba'athist Iraq of the 1970s, freedom was a fantasy you could think of only to yourself, as those who spoke in any way, shape, or form with the slightest hint of opposing the Ba'ath government were severely punished or vanished all together. In fact I think that for some, it might have even been frightening just to think silently about freedom.

Born in Iraq, I have my roots there, and I lived there long enough to remember it and love it. Yet I came to the United States young enough to learn everything else that I know and adapt quickly to living in America and blend into my new environment. I am privileged to have had such an unusual life experience, which has given me a deep understanding and appreciation of both cultures and both countries. All of these things are dear to me and I would like to share them with everyone. I have poured it all into the pages of this book because I care that the people of these two countries, whom I both love, understand each other and get along. I have shared with you in this book what I know about Iraq and the United States over a lifetime of experience in both places. The "here" and "there" are mixed and interchangeable for me.

* * *

Today there is a large Iraqi American community in the United States. All of these Iraqis arrived under different circumstances. Essentially they fall into three groups: first, the pre–1991 Gulf War — those who came to the U.S. during the 1970s and 1980s (even some preceding the 1970s, although they are fewer in number); second, the post–1991 Gulf War — those who came as refugees after the 1991 war; and finally, the group who came after the 2003 war, most of whom also came as refugees although many also came in unique circumstances under special programs, and they are still arriving.

The experience of the first group is vastly different from that of the latter two. This distinction of the experiences of Iraqis based on when they came to the United States and the circumstances under which they came is important. Nearly all who came in the 1970s and early 1980s came as students or professionals under non-war conditions, some even before the Iran–Iraq war. Many of these people were from upper middle class families. They came for educational or professional reasons and were initially supported by their families' expense and efforts. Most of these people came young, in their early twenties; only a few were in their teens like myself. There were also those who came as adult professionals and settled, established their lives and had their children in the United States. These people settled in different states and assimilated individually or as small groups in various towns. They did not exist as one large group in a town or a state. They were dispersed throughout the United States. These people are old now.

Most of the Iraqis who came after the 1991 war and the 2003 war fled Iraq as refugees. They are from various socioeconomic groups and of diverse professional backgrounds. Some among them are uneducated. In times of war, just as during natural disasters, socioeconomic class does not really matter; all are living through a crisis. That is why the Iraqis who came as refugees are of all socioeconomic classes and of all ages. You even saw children and elderly people among them.

I cherish and respect everyone's story, and I hope this book is one of many that will talk about the experiences of Iraqi Americans and what it meant for them to leave Iraq and come to the U.S. The experiences I have described, however, mostly reflect the experience of those who were in the United States from the early 1980s, since I am a part of that group. Our experience is very significant: Of all Iraqi immigrants, we have been in the U.S. the longest time and thus we have experienced living in the United States the most. Newer immigrants do not have that experience yet. In addition, having been in the United States as a teenager, I was even more strongly influenced by American values and lifestyle because

177

I was so young. And because I had no direct guidance and my parents were far away and not accessible, I more or less became my own guide. I used my Iraqi values and whatever new things I learned in the U.S. as my guide to navigate the world. This has led me to great experiences and has given me the most amazing life. I am grateful for that.

NOTES

1. Winter in Baghdad in recent years seems surprisingly mild with only a few cold days in December and January and some in February. When I was growing up in Baghdad in the 1970s winter was harsh and brutally cold and lasted from November until early or mid–February. However, Iraqi homes are not designed to preserve energy well, and even in these relatively mild temperatures it is often colder inside the homes than outside. Everything gets cold — the walls, the ceiling, the floors — and there is always a draft.

Epilogue

In this book, I have tried to draw a picture of the situation in the current Iraq. I have considered what is right and what is wrong, how to fix what is wrong, and why it's important to fix it quickly. I have brought forth in this book a small part of the current situation and recent history of Iraq that I know very well, a history that is enmeshed in myself and that I strove to capture and preserve from loss. I have tried my best to diagnose what is wrong with what was supposed to be a wonderful transition to democracy.

Many years from now, this book can give a picture of what was going on in Iraq and how much I and others tried to change it for the better. Sometimes we succeeded and other times we failed. When future generations wonder what happened during those turbulent years — why chaos prevailed, and why incompetent people were allowed to lead, and where on earth were the wise of this era — I hope they will find some answers in this book. I would like the future generations to know that there were sincere people who worked with honesty and professionalism and wanted to make things better in Iraq.

* * *

But I have also shared my incredible experience of being an Iraqi American, living a life that is a blend of these two great cultures. I have sought to convey what it means and how it feels to be someone like me, between two generations and between two cultures, understanding them both and loving them both and enhancing the understanding between them. I have given you a taste of what it is like now in Iraq and how I adjusted thirty years later — what was difficult, what was awkward, and what was funny or sad.

I feel it is important that my experience is registered and preserved because not many people know of it, and not many people have had a similar experience. My unique experience is what allows me to speak to Iraqis about the United States and to speak to Americans about Iraq. It is what I can try to use to help Iraqis understand and appreciate Americans and Americans understand and appreciate Iraqis. I hope that my story is an inspiration to many people around the world.

I intended this book for Americans, Iraqis, Iraqi Americans, and Iraqis in the Diaspora who may want to come back to Iraq — not only to help Iraq but, like me, to also jump into their own sea of memories and sensations. The book is also for Americans and Iraqis whose lives have been intertwined by living with the consequences of the war — consequences they will continue to live with for decades to come. Further, I hope that this book will be a delight to Americans and others going to Iraq as experts, researchers, and diplomats as well as to decision makers in the United States, Iraq and all over the world.

I hope that this book will plant the seeds of understanding for Iraqis and Americans so that we can have the hope of healing our societies from the injuries we have caused each other. This way we can move away from misunderstandings and look forward to a good future together. By establishing understanding and abolishing ignorance on both sides, we can build bridges of hope and friendship and mend broken hearts.

* * *

There is a solution to Iraq's predicament. There is a way to make this democracy a success. First, politicians must stay in their domain of political squabble and leave room for professionals and experts do their work. Professionals and experts must run the various agencies and ministries so that a decent life may be attained for people. Only technocrats specialized in various fields can solve the chronic daily problems affecting electric power, employment, security, health care, sanitation and so on. Further, Iraq must begin to appreciate its treasures and jewels: its experts, scientists, teachers, volunteers, expatriates and children, as well as its historical and archeological sites. I hope thousands of *resilient* and *unrelenting* expatriates will go to Iraq, find something they can help in, and just do it: infuse knowledge, fresh ideas and skills wherever they land. This is the only solution for Iraq, and as Iraqis say, *inshallah* (God willing).

Index

Numbers in ***bold italics*** indicate pages with photographs.